A GI in the Ardennes

First published in Belgium in 2017 by Editions Racine
Republished in the English Language in Great Britain in 2020 by
Pen & Sword Military
An imprint of
Pen & Sword Books Limited
Yorkshire - Philadelphia

© 2017, Editions Racine. For the original edition.
Original title: Le quotidien des GI. Le bataille des Ardennes

© 2019, Pen and Sword Books Limited. For the English edition

ISBN 978 1 52675 6 183

Printed and bound in India
by Replika Press Pvt. Ltd

Pen & Sword Books Limited incorporates the imprints of Atlas,
Archaeology, Aviation, Discovery, Family History, Fiction, History,
Maritime, Military, Military Classics, Politics, Select, Transport, True
Crime, Air World, Frontline Publishing, Leo Cooper, Remember When,
Seaforth Publishing, The Praetorian Press, Wharncliffe Local History,
Wharncliffe Transport, Wharncliffe True Crime and White Owl.

For a complete list of Pen & Sword titles please contact
PEN & SWORD BOOKS LIMITED
47 Church Street, Barnsley, South Yorkshire S70 2AS, United Kingdom
E-mail: enquiries@pen-and-sword.co.uk
Website: www.pen-and-sword.co.uk

Or

PEN AND SWORD BOOKS
1950 Lawrence Rd, Havertown, PA 19083, USA
E-mail: Uspen-and-sword@casematepublishers.com
Website: www.penandswordbooks.com

A GI in the Ardennes

The Battle of the Bulge

Denis Hambucken

Pen & Sword
MILITARY

Table of Contents

The Battle of the Bulge

The Liberation of Western Europe

With the success of *Operation Overlord* in Normandy on June 6, 1944, the Allies secure a firm foothold in Western Europe. It takes two months of relentless fighting to break out of Normandy's hedgerows but then German forces seem to collapse. On August 15 the Allies launch *Operation Dragoon* on the French Riviera, an amphibious assault similar to that of Normandy, but smaller in scale. Threatened with being cut off, the Germans withdraw. Paris is liberated on August 25 and Brussels only a week later.

Christian de Marcken is sixteen years old in 1944. With his mother and some of his siblings, he observes a column of retreating Germans near Rixensart, Belgium. Short of gasoline, the Germans resort to pulling their trucks with draft horses. When Mrs. de Marcken and the children notice a flight of American P-47 Thunderbolt ground attack fighter airplanes, they move away quickly. From a safe distance they observe the aircraft swooping to the sound of gunfire, explosions and the cries of horses. Christian vividly remembers gleaming streams of machine gun bullets cutting through the sky. When they return to the scene later, hoping to cut meat from the dead horses, charred vehicles litter the road. The Germans have evacuated the wounded and the dead, but Christian discovers that they have overlooked a helmet with a decapitated head still in it. He recalls: "At that time, I could not get horrified. There was so much hatred in me." News of rapidly advancing British and American troops spreads rapidly. Christian's parents take enormous risks hiding an illicit radio behind a pile of firewood in their house. The children spread throughout the large house as lookouts while the parents listen to BBC reports. The encouraging news emboldens resistance groups eager to secure their small share of glory. On September 1944 in Hody, Belgium, partisans shoot and kill two Germans on a motorcycle and sidecar then leave the bodies on the street. This ill-inspired and sloppy operation does nothing to hasten the liberation of the town, but it prompts the Das Reich SS Division to shoot all the adult male villagers and burn down much of the town in retaliation.[1]

Allied convoys spread elation as they progress from town to town. Villagers flood the streets to welcome their liberators and to celebrate the end of four years of occupation. Al York of the 309th Engineer Combat Battalion echoes the sentiment of many soldiers: "You couldn't ask for better people. I'd say they were the most friendly of all the people. Even more friendly than the Dutch." René Mamèche is six years old in 1944. He lives in Temploux, a small town near Namur, Belgium where his parents run a bakery. He fondly remembers the arrival of the Americans in the afternoon of September 3, 1944: "It was a day of unbelievable rapture! Acclamations, hugs, kisses, flowers! The villagers opened their best bottles!" René is impressed by the brand new vehicles and equipment and by the vibrant, tall and affable young Americans: "The soldiers were very nice with the kids, particularly the black soldiers: They readily stopped and they gave us candy." The U.S. Army soon establishes a camp in town and undertakes the construction of a large airfield. René recalls that there was surprisingly little security around American installations and that overall, locals got along well with their American guests in spite of a few incidents: "There was a little friction due to relationships with local girls. Some of the soldiers had a tendency to drink too much, they would abandon their vehicles in town, sometimes right over the tramway rails." René remembers three Army bakers who arranged to use his parents' bakery to prepare cakes and pies for Thanksgiving.

Charles Mernier is ten years old at the time. He gets his first glimpse of American soldiers during the decidedly less dramatic liberation of Assenois. At the sound of the church bells, Charles runs to town just in time to see two soldiers in a jeep. They drive by, stop for a while then turn back.

The Allies' advance is so much faster than expected, that supplies cannot

keep up. Railroads and harbors have been damaged by Allied bombings or by retreating Germans. General Omar Bradley wrote in his autobiography that on average, the twenty-eight divisions in France and Belgium consume a staggering 20,000 tons of supplies every single day.[2] An elaborate trucking operation known as the *Red Ball Express* (See page 62) is put in place to keep supplies flowing between the coast of Normandy and the front line, now advancing through the Netherlands, Belgium and Luxembourg. But supply shortages continue to hinder Allied progress. On September 4, British forces assisted by local partisans seize the Belgian port of Antwerp nearly intact. The harbor – one of Europe's largest – has the potential to solve supply problems. But Field Marshal Bernard Montgomery neglects to clear the estuary until the end of November. Instead, eager to be first to cross the Rhine, Montgomery plans the ill-fated *Operation Market Garden*. Launched on September 17, the ambitious operation hinges on the largest airborne deployment in history in an attempt to circumvent the defensive "Siegfried" line through the Netherlands. *Operation Market Garden* fails due to poor planning, hurried preparations, bad intelligence, bad weather and unexpectedly strong German resistance.

On October 21, after twenty days of fierce house-to-house fighting, Aachen becomes the first major German city to fall to the Americans. Further south, the Hurtgen forest, an area of less than fifty square kilometers is the object of particularly protracted and fruitless fighting. The cold rain and autumn mud usher in a general moroseness. Divisions like the 36th that had advanced ten miles per day in September have come nearly to a standstill.[3] Instances of desertions, self-inflicted wounds, negligent trench foot or lagging behind, rise sharply. Hopes of a victory before Christmas have dissipated.

The German Perspective

It has become evident to anyone with a realistic grasp of the situation that Germany's defeat is ineluctable. Hitler is fighting a war on three expansive fronts. He has been evicted from North Africa, much of Italy, France, Belgium and Luxembourg. Axis dictator Benito Mussolini has been overthrown and brutally executed. The Russians, backed by American supplies, are doggedly fighting their way across Poland. British and Canadian forces are pushing into the Netherlands. Allied planes are bombing Germany at will.

From Hitler's contorted perspective however, all is not lost. His entourage does its best to avoid his famous accusations of defeatism. Rather that present realistic assessments of the situation, they prefer to emphasize positive news and optimistic forecasts. This feeds into Hitler's inflated impression of his remaining military strength. He has a strong sense of destiny and is confident that somehow, fate will intervene in his favor, just as it seemingly has in July when he miraculously survived a bombing plot at his *Wolfsschanze* (Wolf Lair) headquarters. Hitler and his SS leadership hold that the Aryan purity of German soldiers makes them inherently superior to Anglo-American soldiers. They view the industrial might of the United States as an unfair and cowardly advantage and believe that British and American infantrymen could not hold their own without the support of their air forces. The

Photo: Inhabitants of Rongy, Belgium turn out to cheer the arrival of an American column on September 3, 1944. Left: This scaled version of the famous "Mannekenpis" statue was purchased in Brussels in 1944 by Bill Gast, a tank driver of the 743rd Tank Battalion.

loss of territory has come with a few advantages. While the Allies' supply lines are stretched to their breaking point, Germany's have become shorter and more secure. Under the direction of Albert Speer, Germany's war industry has been streamlined and decentralized in such ways that production, with the exception of fuel, is reaching record levels in spite of relentless bombings. German forces now enjoy the home advantage on the western front. They are regrouping behind the *Westwall*, a line of fortifications and tank obstacles. Artillery becomes more concentrated as it retreats and regroups. Allies on German soil can no longer count on assistance from friendly populations and partisans. Hitler believes that if only he could regain the initiative, he might reverse his country's disastrous course. No single offensive against the vast Russians front can have a lasting impact, but Hitler sees an opportunity in the west. He reasons that while it will not win the war outright, a major offensive might start a chain of events that could lead the Allies to reconsider their demand for unconditional surrender. Or perhaps

it would buy Germany enough time to rebuild the *Luftwaffe* with new jet fighters or for the V1 and V2 vengeance weapons to fulfill their potential.

Wacht Am Rhein

On September 16, 1944, at his daily conference, Hitler announces to a small circle among his General Staff his decision to go on the offensive in the west. He has selected the Ardennes as a launch area and Antwerp as the main objective. Antwerp, which was lost to the Allies only a few weeks earlier, is sure to become a key port of entry for supplies. Hitler knows the Ardennes to be thinly defended. The forested terrain and late fall weather will provide cover from aerial attacks and reconnaissance during both the buildup phase and the operation itself. Furthermore, the path from the Ardennes to Antwerp roughly marks the boundary between American forces to the south and British and Canadian forces to the north, therefore the offensive will likely exacerbate the growing tensions between the British and the Americans,

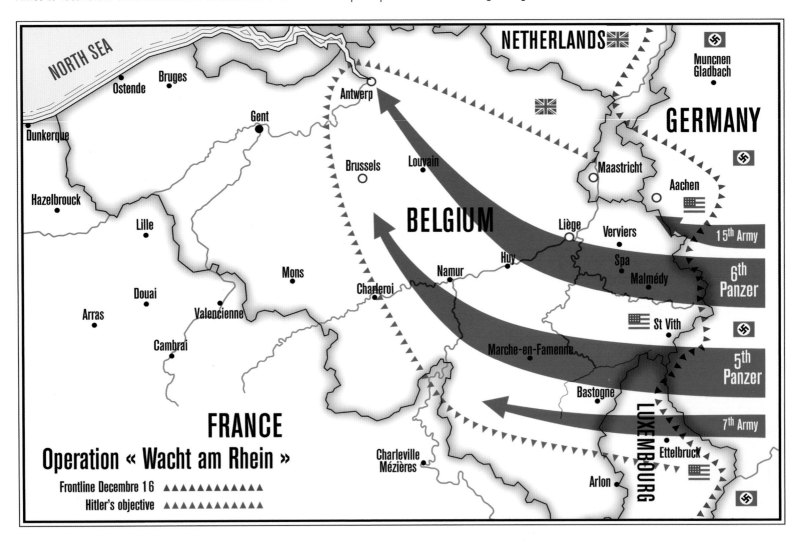

and make a coordinated response more complicated. Hitler's Generals deem the plan unrealistic given Germany's depleted troops and crippling fuel shortages and propose less ambitious objectives, but Hitler accepts no compromise. The operation, deceptively named *Wacht am Rhein* (Defense of the Rhine), is to be launched in November. It calls for four armies to attack on a front that extends some 85 miles from Monschau to Echternach along the border with Belgium and Luxembourg. Vehicles will have to be refueled at captured American depots along the way. *Operation Greif* (Griffon) will infiltrate commando units disguised as American troops ahead of the main forces to secure important bridges before American forces can destroy them. The offensive also includes *Operation Bodenplatte* (Baseplate), a series of coordinated air raids on Allied airfields, and *Operation Stösser* (Auk), a nighttime drop of about 1,300 paratroopers to secure a key crossroad at Baraque Michel and block Allied reinforcements from the north. The Fifth Panzer Army under Hasso Von Manteuffel and the Sixth Panzer army under Sepp Dietrich are to cross the river Meuse, then turn north towards Brussels and Antwerp while the fifteenth and the seventh Armies will protect the northern and southern flanks respectively.

The "Ghost Front"

Many American accounts of the Battle of the Bulge erroneously refer to the Ardennes as a mountainous region. The particularly cold and snowy winter of 1944 reinforces the impression of a harsh, rugged environment, but there are in fact no mountains in the Ardennes. The region is a succession of plateaus crisscrossed by deep, sinuous valleys. The landscape is a patchwork of deciduous forests, dense coniferous plantations, and farmland - mostly pastures - dotted here and there with picturesque ancient villages. There are no major urban centers. Towns are generally isolated groups of stone buildings agglomerated around ancient churches and fortified farmhouses. From a military perspective, when compared to surrounding regions, the Ardennes is difficult terrain that favors defensive tactics. Steep valleys and forests confine traffic to key river crossings and a limited network of narrow, sinuous roads. Neighboring towns are often connected by a single road. Eisenhower is little interested in the Ardennes as he deems regions to the north and south much more suitable for offensive actions. General Hodges' 1st Army covers the area. It is part of the 12th Army Group sector that stretches from Aachen to the Lorraine region of France. Because the Ardennes front

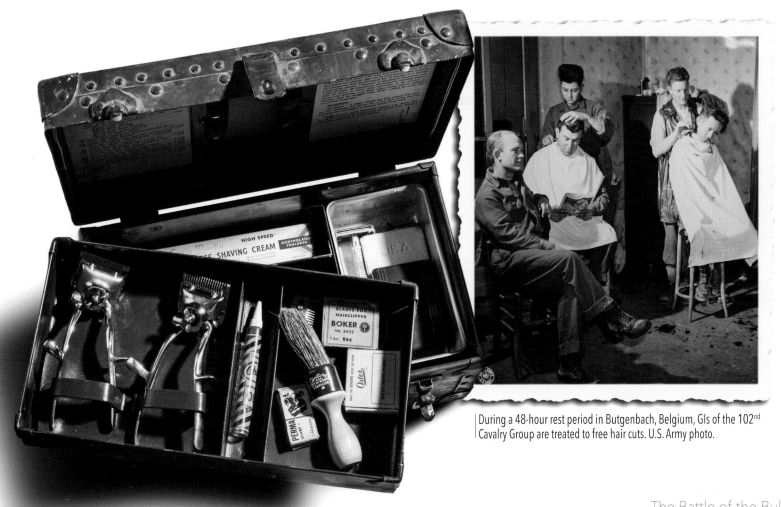

During a 48-hour rest period in Butgenbach, Belgium, GIs of the 102nd Cavalry Group are treated to free hair cuts. U.S. Army photo.

is stagnant and quiet, it becomes known as the "Ghost Front". The 1st Army, having just lost some 30,000 men in the fruitless battle of the Hurtgen forest, is sent there to rest and to acclimate its fresh replacements. Troop concentration is highest between Aachen and Elsenborn where Eisenhower is planning his next big push into Germany. Other areas are thinly defended; some near the Losheim gap are only patrolled by jeeps during the day. Omar Bradley would later insist that it had been a calculated risk.

German Preparations

Hitler understands that success will hinge on two conditions. First, the element of surprise must be preserved at all cost and the offensive has to adhere to a brisk timetable to prevent the Allies from regrouping and reorganizing. Second, the weather must be such that Allied airplanes remain grounded. To prevent leaks or intercepts, Hitler imposes strict telephone and radio silence. Knowledge of the operation is restricted to a small circle of high ranking officers, all sworn to secrecy under penalty of death. Their movements and communications are closely monitored by *Gestapo* agents. The concentration of troops, equipment, fuel and ammunition under strict secrecy, represents an enormous logistical challenge. Troops, tanks, and artillery are brought in under cover of darkness from as far away as Poland and Norway on a rail network that is relentlessly bombed by Allied planes. Arrived near their assembly areas in close proximity to American lines, they are carefully dispersed and camouflaged. To avoid telltale smoke plumes, troops are issued charcoal instead of firewood. The bulk of the troops would only be informed of the offensive the day before it is launched. In spite of the Germans' best efforts, some American troops and civilians notice unusual or suspicious activity, but their reports are downplayed or dismissed. As he accompanied a six-men patrol from the 38th Cavalry Group somewhere east

of Bullingen, 1st Lt. Wesley Ross observed: "Trees were being cut down with saws and axes, and tanks and other heavy motorized equipment were moving around over straw-covered trails to muffle their sounds. While watching this activity from a concealed position two hundred yards away on the opposite side of the canyon, we listened to the big tank engines for some time and sensed that something unusual was afoot.[4]" Bill Campbell and his buddy "Rosie" of the 28th Infantry Division are manning a forward observation post. When they report increased activity with numerous trucks and tanks, the response from their headquarter is: "These must be ours." To which they replied: "When did we start wearing gray uniforms?"

The Offensive

At 5:30 in the morning of December 16, American guard details up and down the 90 mile front notice distant flashes of German artillery. At first, sleepy GIs, well protected in their dugouts, are not overly concerned by the barrage, but they become alarmed as it grows unusually intense and persistent. In some sectors, American positions become illuminated by anti-aircraft spotlights reflected on low clouds to create a sort of artificial moonlight. Overwhelming numbers of *Volksgrenadiers*, armed with automatic weapons emerge from the woods. Harry Martin Jr. of the 106th Infantry Division wrote: "They acted like they were drunk or on drugs. They came over the hill screaming and shrieking [...] I was panic-stricken. I felt like my entire life force had left my body. I was already dead and I was fighting like a zombie. Sheer panic had set in, causing me to fire my rifle without thinking or aiming.[5]"

The first wave of *Volksgrenadiers* is soon followed by a second wave of *Panzergrenadiers* and their armored vehicles. Chuck Wenc of the 106th Infantry Division recalls that everybody feared the Tiger tank: "If you were in a foxhole you could hear it and you got scared shitless. They sound big and heavy. You can tell it's a tiger tank by the gun, as big as a telephone pole!" At the sight of the massive tank, Chuck ducks in his foxhole. He recalls: "There was another guy behind me. Our holes were maybe a hundred feet apart.[...]. Maybe he had not seen me, or he confused me. The tank was over me and I thought: 'Holly Christ!' Then I waited a little while. I popped my head up; he was going away from me. He gets to where the other GI was. He skidded. Buried him alive. The guy was gone."

German artillery destroys telephone lines, and radios are unreliable due to

This photo was taken in Honsfeld, probably on December 17. Honsfeld is likely the site of the first massacre of American prisoners. One of the Germans is seen tying the shoes that he just took from an dead American soldier lying face down in the mud. U.S. Army photo.

These two photos were taken a few minutes apart. They show SS soldiers advancing along a destroyed column of American vehicles. One of the men is armed with the *Sturmgewehr 44*, the first modern assault rifle in the world. U.S. Army photo.

the hilly terrain, weather and German jamming. Spotty communication leads to confusion and prevents rear echelons from forming a clear picture of the developing situation, each unit believing that it is the object of a localized attack. East of St. Vith, two of the three regiments of the newly formed 106th Infantry Division become encircled. They are unsure if they have permission to withdraw and are under the impression that reinforcements will soon reach them. Under fire from all sides and low on supplies, some 7,000 men surrender in what will stand as the largest American reverse of the entire war in Europe.

Overall, Americans are outnumbered three to one. In many sectors, they are outnumbered six to one.[6] They suffer heavy losses of both men and equipment and have no choice but to fall back. In some places, the panic is contagious. As they flee westward, battered GIs and civilian refugees spreading news of an overwhelming German force create a snowball effect. Groups of Americans who have stood their ground and survived, find themselves isolated behind enemy lines with many wounded comrades and few supplies. Chuck Wenc is among the men of the 106th Division that have evaded capture. He remembers: "We were hit very hard. Then the Lieutenant said: 'Everybody

on his own! Just pull back! Pull back everybody!' [...] We wound up with all kinds of outfits, I didn't know half the guys." Chuck fights with the 7th Armored for a while, then the 82nd Airborne: "We fought in groups of maybe five or six men. We're a platoon and we held up a company of Germans, just because we wanted to and we had the guts to do it, but nobody told us we had to do this."

The Northern Sector

The sixth Panzer Army under *SS-Oberst-Gruppenführer* Josef "Sepp" Dietrich covers the northern sector with the most direct route to Antwerp. The spearhead of Dietrich's army is *Kampfgruppe Peiper*. Named after its commander, *SS-Obersturmbannführer* Joachim Peiper of the 1st SS Panzer Division, *Kampfgruppe Peiper* is the most powerful, best-equipped and most mobile task force of the entire offensive. With some five thousand foot soldiers, more than 100 tanks,[9] plus supporting vehicles and artillery, Peiper's column stretches some 25 kilometers.[8] Peiper has been offered the best routes into Belgium through the Losheim Gap, but he is soon forced into detours and delays. The elite division of *Fallschirmjäger* tasked with breaching

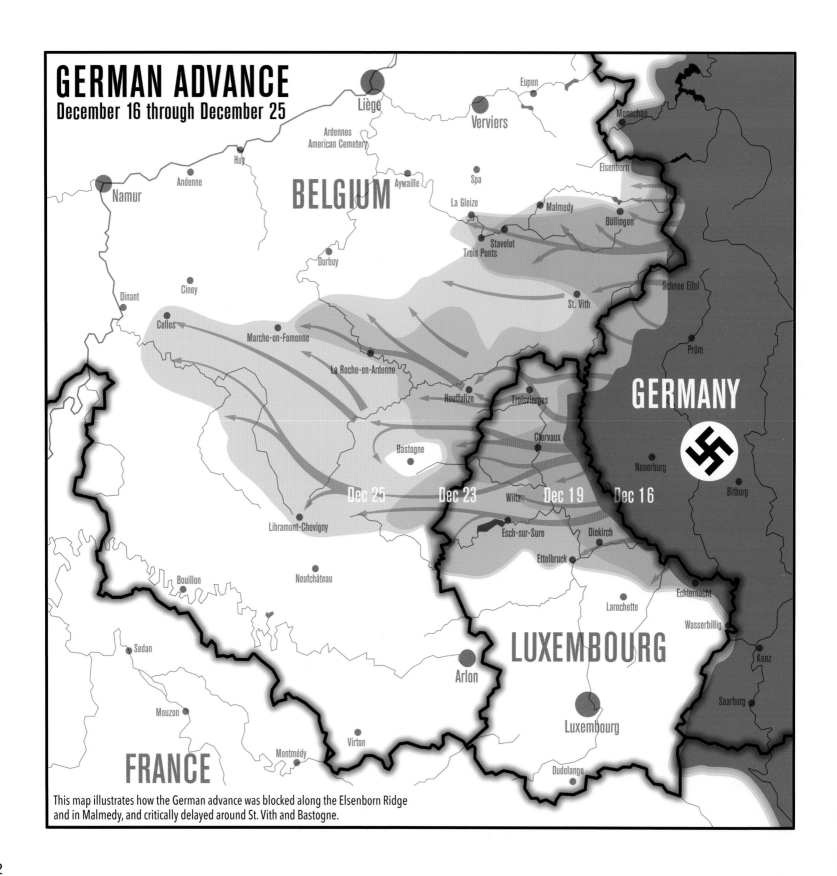

GERMAN ADVANCE
December 16 through December 25

BELGIUM

GERMANY

LUXEMBOURG

FRANCE

Liège
Eupen
Monschau
Verviers
Ardennes
American Cemetery
Elsenborn
Huy
Spa
Aywaille
Andenne
La Gleize
Malmedy
Büllingen
Namur
Stavelot
Trois Ponts
Durbuy
Schnee Eifel
Ciney
St. Vith
Dinant
Prüm
Celles
Marche-en-Famenne
La Roche-en-Ardenne
Houffalize
Troisvierges
Clervaux
Neuerburg
Bastogne
Bitburg
Dec 25
Dec 23
Wiltz
Dec 19
Dec 16
Libramont-Chevigny
Esch-sur-Sure
Diekirch
Ettelbruck
Neufchâteau
Bouillon
Larochette
Echternacht
Wasserbillig
Sedan
Konz
Arlon
Luxembourg
Mouzon
Saarburg
Virton
Montmédy
Dudelange

This map illustrates how the German advance was blocked along the Elsenborn Ridge
and in Malmedy, and critically delayed around St. Vith and Bastogne.

12

the American lines ahead of Peiper is held up in Lanzerath for an entire day by a twenty-two-men American platoon (See Page 119). *Operation* Stösser, an airborne operation tasked with securing the Baraque Michel crossroad north of Malmedy to prevent American reinforcement from the north, proves a dismal failure. Both the paratroopers and their pilots are poorly trained. The drop is too scattered due to poor navigation, reduced visibility and strong wind. Of the 1,300 *Fallschirmjäger* only about three hundred reach their assembly point; most have lost much of their heavy equipment. The failure of *Operation Stösser* and stubborn American opposition on the Elsenborn ridge leaves Peiper's flanks and supply lines vulnerable and forces him onto less favorable routes further west.

Peiper and his SS leave a trail of massacres of Belgian civilians and American prisoners of war, probably in response to Hitler's orders that the attack be conducted with such brutality that "A wave of fright and terror must precede the troops.[3]" On December 17, Peiper's men execute 84 American prisoners in old blood near Malmedy (see page 126). Peiper and his SS men have already distinguished themselves for their ruthlessness on the Russian front, but on the western front, such massacres represent a shocking escalation in brutality. Before the day is out, news of the "Malmedy Massacre" reaches front line soldiers throughout the Ardennes. GIs everywhere vow to avoid surrender at all cost and thereafter, few Germans would be taken prisoner, particularly if wearing SS uniforms. Due to Germany's severe gasoline shortages, Peiper has not been allocated enough fuel to reach Antwerp. His success depends on capturing American fuel dumps along the way. While

fighting on the Elsenborn Ridge, Joseph Kiss of the 2nd infantry division notices that German soldiers carry an unusual piece of equipment: "Every fourth or fifth German carried a hose about five feet long and a half inch wide. We wondered why. Then it dawned on me: It was to siphon gas from disabled vehicles.[10]" Brief breaks in the cloud cover allow American fighter-bombers to inflict some damage, and just as importantly, they give away Peiper's exact location. Engineers are able to destroy key bridges ahead of his advance, forcing him into further detours and delays. Peiper makes it as far as Stoumont on December 19, but the following day his supply lines are cut off and he is confronted by stiff opposition by men and tanks from the 82nd Airborne and 30th Infantry Divisions. Suffering heavy losses and running out of fuel and ammunition, *Kampfgruppe Peiper* pulls back to La Gleize. On December 24, when resupply and reinforcements fail to reach him, Peiper abandons his vehicles and walks back to the German lines with fewer than 800 of his men.

Bastogne and the Southern Sector

In the southern sector, Manteufel's 5th Panzer Army slams into the 28th Infantry Division. The Americans are overwhelmed, but in towns like Clervaux,

This image of one of *Kampfgruppe Knittel* command cars was captured in Kaiserbaracke on December 18, 1944. U.S. Army photo.

Weiler and Wiltz they put up a determined fight and succeed in delaying the German advance. The battle of Clervaux becomes known as the Luxembourg Alamo when about a hundred men of the 110th Infantry Regiment hold a castle overnight after the rest of the town has been conceded.

After the first few chaotic days, a more dependable situational map begins to emerge. It is clear that the Germans have organized their forces into two main prongs with the objective of reaching the Meuse and that Bastogne is a key waypoint. On December 19, General Eisenhower meets with his senior generals in Verdun. He tries to set the tone with his opening remark: "The present situation is to be regarded as one of opportunity for us and not of disaster. There will be only cheerful faces at this conference table." When Eisenhower asks General George Patton how much time he needs to prepare a counteroffensive from the south, Patton replies in his characteristically boastful way that he will attack within 48 hours.

The 101st and the 82nd Airborne Divisions are held in reserve near Reims, France to recuperate after their action in the Netherlands during *Operation Market Garden*. On December 17, they are rushed to the Ardennes. Herb Adams of the 82nd Airborne Division remembers a frigid overnight trip in open trucks. The men are packed so tightly that there is no room to sit, and the trucks only stop long enough to refuel or swap drivers: "Now it's midnight again and you haven't had a chance to sleep (in 24 hours). You jumped off the goddamned trucks, now we had to walk. I think it was about 8 miles and you immediately go into attack against the Germans." While the 82nd ends up near Stoumont to confront Peiper, the 101st improvises a defensive perimeter around Bastogne, just before the town becomes surrounded on December 21. The bulk of the panzer forces bypasses Bastogne to forge ahead towards Marche-en-Famenne. The defenders of Bastogne under Brigadier General Antony McAuliffe are cut off, severely outnumbered, and critically low on winter gear, ammunition and medical supplies. On December 22, General Von Lüttwitz issues an ultimatum threatening to annihilate Bastogne with artillery if the Americans do not surrender. General McAuliffe famously responds: "Nuts". The heroic defiance and the colorful response set against the bittersweet romance of a wartime Christmas are prime material for news editors. "Bastogne, the bastion of the battered bastards" becomes a symbol of American stoicism. Captain Jack Prior, a doctor attached to the 10th Armored Division would later write: "We never had any idea of the importance of this battle, thinking it was just another town. Its importance did not dawn upon us until one day we hooked up a radio to a vehicular battery and heard the BBC in London paying tribute to the 'Gallant defenders of Bastogne.' They compared this battle to Waterloo, Gettysburg, and Verdun.[11]"

Hitler too, turns his attention to Bastogne. Since hopes of crossing the Meuse are dissipating, he is eager to secure a token victory and crush what has become the symbol of American resilience. He redirects troops from the failed northern sector towards Bastogne, but the following day the sky clears. At long last, eager American and British airplanes jump into the fray, bombing German supply lines, attacking armored columns and dropping supplies. Dr. Jack Prior wrote: "Hundreds of C-47s droned over Bastogne and

Refugees pass through bomb-ravaged Bastogne on December 30, 1944. U.S. Army photo. The German Gewehr 43 semi-automatic rifle is nicknamed the "German Garand" by American soldiers, although its design is inspired primarily by the Soviet SVT 40 rifle.

8 K BASTOGNE

When the tide of war swings back in favor of the Allies in late December, demoralized German soldiers surrender en mass. They bet that if they survive the first few very tense minutes, they will be treated well in American prisoner of war camps. U.S. National Archives photo.

multicolored parachutes fell to earth – each color representing a category of supplies. Food, ammunition, blankets, medical items were eagerly gathered.[11]" The first elements of Patton's 3rd Army reach Bastogne on December 26, and the siege is definitively broken the following day.

Leading German forces that have bypassed Bastogne make it as far as Celles, only a few miles from the city of Dinant on the Meuse river. But strong British and American defenses around the bridges make further progress impossible. The German offensive has reached its high-water mark and has exhausted its gasoline supplies. The Allies have stabilized the front and regained control of the situation, but the battle is far from over. It will take a full month of fighting in worsening weather to squeeze the stubborn German troops out of the Ardennes and to return the front line to where it had been in early December.

The final score

Casualty figures are disputed and will never be know precisely. Americans suffered an estimated 80,000 casualties including approximately 19,000 killed and as many missing or taken prisoner. German casualties estimates

range from 70,000 to 140,000. While the United States manages to absorb these losses relatively quickly, Germany comes out severely and irreparably depleted.

Given the overall balance of power in Europe in the fall of 1944, it seems obvious that the best that Hitler's Germany could have achieved was a modest setback in the Allies' unstoppable advance to Berlin. When Hitler devised his plan for the Ardennes offensive, he likely had no clear strategic objective, beyond regaining the initiative. In his volume of the US Army official history about the Battle of the Bulge, historian Hugh Cole wrote: "It seems more probable, from all that is known of Hitler's thought processes in these last months of his life, that [...] the German decision was not between war and peace but between defense and attack.[6]" The enormous Allied losses in the city of Aachen and the Hurtgen forest attest to the effectiveness of German forces in well-prepared defensive positions. It is therefore likely that by sticking his neck out in an all-out offensive, Hitler precipitated Germany's fate and perhaps spared the Allies even greater losses. In the Verdun meeting of December 19, General Patton had famously boasted: "This time the Kraut stuck his head in the meat grinder, and this time I've got hold of the handle.[12]" Perhaps Hitler's biggest miscalculation was the contempt he held for the average American soldier. The success of the offensive hinged on an ambitious timeline that could only be met if disheartened American soldiers gave in to panic or disgust. But for various reasons, enough of them found the fortitude to stand their ground. Or perhaps as Audie Murphy wrote in his memoir, they: "Lacked the guts to take being thought cowards.[7]"

The GI Uniform and Equipment

This man is wearing the chevrons of a Technical Sergeant, a non-commissioned officer grade that typically leads a platoon of twelve men into combat. The War Department updates the soldiers' equipment and uniform several times through the war, but new equipment is introduced gradually as old stock runs out. As a result, many soldiers sport assortments of various vintages, some predating the First World War. This, plus a natural penchant for informality sometimes lends the U.S. Army a relaxed, some might say ragtag appearance. This sergeant is equipped with an M-1928 haversack, and M-1911 entrenching tool.

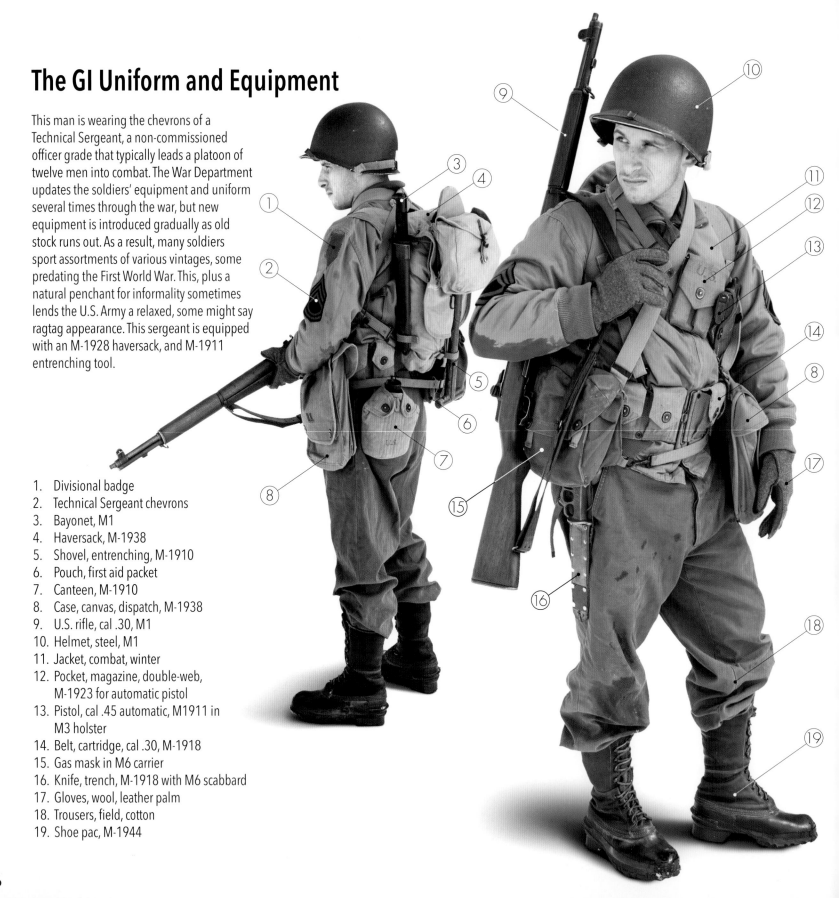

1. Divisional badge
2. Technical Sergeant chevrons
3. Bayonet, M1
4. Haversack, M-1938
5. Shovel, entrenching, M-1910
6. Pouch, first aid packet
7. Canteen, M-1910
8. Case, canvas, dispatch, M-1938
9. U.S. rifle, cal .30, M1
10. Helmet, steel, M1
11. Jacket, combat, winter
12. Pocket, magazine, double-web, M-1923 for automatic pistol
13. Pistol, cal .45 automatic, M1911 in M3 holster
14. Belt, cartridge, cal .30, M-1918
15. Gas mask in M6 carrier
16. Knife, trench, M-1918 with M6 scabbard
17. Gloves, wool, leather palm
18. Trousers, field, cotton
19. Shoe pac, M-1944

Between November 1942 and July 1943, the Quartermaster Board tests improved combat clothing and equipment with the goal of developing a standardized set that can be distributed across many branches of service and that is adaptable to a wide range of climates. The result is the M1943 uniform worn by this infantryman. Among the most significant upgrades are the thigh-length combat jacket, larger backpack, improved entrenching shovel and cuffed buckle combat boots. This man is armed with a BAR (See page 36). For protection against the cold, he is wearing the standard-issue wool and leather gloves, a knit wool beanie under his helmet, and a scarf hand-knitted by an American Red Cross volunteer.

1. Helmet , steel, M1 with net
2. Cap, wool, knit, M-1941
3. Jacket, field, M-1943
4. Scarf, hand-knitted by Red Cross volunteer
5. Pack, M-1943
6. Belt, magazine, BAR, M-1937
7. Pouch, first aid packet
8. Knife, trench, M3 in M6 scabbard
9. Trousers, field, cotton
10. Boot, service, combat
11. Gloves, wool, leather palm
12 Browning Automatic Rifle, cal .30, M-1918A2
13. Case, cleaning rod, M1
14. Shovel, entrenching, M-1943
15. Gas mask in M6 carrier
16. Canteen, M-1941

The Draft

In 1940, the United States are not yet militarily involved in the war, but the threat grows with each of Hitler's victories in Europe. The War Department undertakes a large expansion and modernization effort. By September, the army's annual budget rises to $8 billion, more than the combined budgets of the previous twenty years[13], with the goal of readying an army of 1.5 million men and a modern Air Force. Forty-six new military camps are established, an ambitious project that requires 400,000 construction workers, 10 million square feet of wallboard, 3,500 carloads of nails and 908,000 gallons of paint.[14] To fill the ranks of the expanded armed forces, the *Selective Training and Service Act* imposes the first peacetime draft in the country's history. Under the new law, men between the ages of 21 and 36 are required to enroll at their local draft board and thereafter carry a *Registration Certificate* (A) as proof of their enrollment. Each registrant receives a summon to a preliminary medical examination and interview (B) to assess his fitness for military service. Soon thereafter, he receives his notice of classification that ranges from 1-A: available for military service, to 4-F: unfit for military service, with various deferments in between, including 3-B: deferred due to occupation essential to the war effort. Candidates usually do their best to conceal any condition or weakness that might disqualify them but many, having grown up during the great depression, show signs of malnutrition or insufficient education, particularly among those coming from poor southern and midwestern states. In parts of the country up to 50% of candidates are rejected for various physical or cognitive deficiencies, including illiteracy, bad teeth, poor eyesight, insufficient height, weight, etc. In some circles, rejected men having received the classification 4-F, are derogatorily referred to as "F'ers", and unfairly stigmatized. From the pool or registrants, annual quotas are selected through a lottery system and inducted into a 12-month (Later 18-month) military service.

Following the Japanese attack on Pearl Harbor and America's subsequent entry into the war, millions of young men volunteer for service. Mandatory enrollment for the draft is expanded to men between 18 and 64 years of age, with only those between the ages of 20 and 44 actually eligible for service. The length of service is increased to the duration of the war plus six months.

Starting in November of 1942, every eligible man is drafted into service as soon as he turns 18. And starting in February of 1944 to expedite and simplify the draft process, candidates are sent directly to an army camp for medical examination and classification. If deemed fit for service, they are inducted immediately.

By the end of the war, 50 million men had registered for the draft, and 10 million of them had been inducted into service.

Young draftees are waiting to board the train that will take them to a military training camp. U.S. Library of Congress photo.

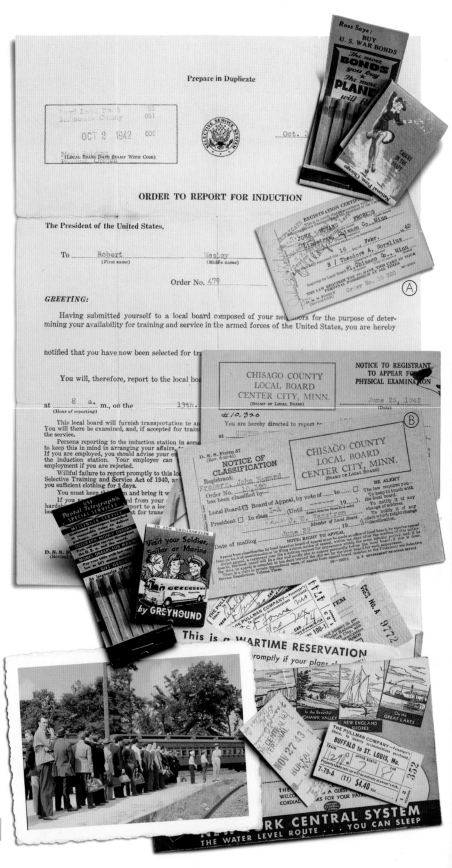

Immunizations

Don Mason of the 743rd Tank Battalion writes on May 9, 1942 during his training at Fort Lewis, Washington: "I was going to write yesterday. But I got a shot for yellow fever and my arm was so sore I could hardly move it. I stayed in bed most all day Sunday. First I would freeze and then I would burn up." John Duquoin of the same battalion writes: "We got our final tetanus shots today. They sure do burn for a couple of hours afterward, but they don't make one as sore or feverish as the typhoid vaccine. We only have one more shot now – yellow fever." Evidently, most soldiers dread the army's long and painful inoculation program, but it would prove very wise. In the squalid conditions of Japanese and German prisoner of war camps, typhus and yellow fever kill tens of thousands of men. Thanks to their immunizations, American prisoners fare better than other nationals.

Dog Tags

Stainless steel identification tags are issued in pairs. In case of injury or death, one tag can be left with the soldier while the other is taken away for administrative purposes. With the help of a pistol-grip press with a built-in roll of carbon paper, the embossed lettering can be imprinted directly onto forms. One of the tags shown above is fitted with a rubber silencer improvised from a segment of a gas mask hose (see page 53) to prevent the tags from jingling. Information on the dog tag includes the soldier's name, serial number, year of induction (44), blood type (A), year of last tetanus inoculation (T 44) and religious denomination (C for Catholic). For fear of mistreatment by Nazis in case of capture, Jewish soldiers often elect to omit the letter H for Hebrew. The serial number starting with 39 indicates that this man is a draftee from the west coast of the United States. As customary in American society, birth names are usually ignored in favor of one or two-syllable nicknames, often contractions of first or last names. Bill Campbell of the 28th Infantry Division is known as "Camby", John McAuliffe of the 87th Infantry Division is known simply as "Mac". If a soldier has red hair, he is likely known as "Red" or "Rusty". If he is particularly thin, he is likely known as "Bones" or "Slim". Victor Sacco of the 552nd Artillery Battalion recalls: "If they didn't know your name it was 'Hey, Joe!' or 'Hey, Mac!'"

"FIRST THING I WANT TO IMPRESS ON YOU MEN, IS THAT YOU AINT FREE TO COME AND GO AT WILL!"

Basic Training

The Army operates 242 training camps distributed throughout the United States.[15] The larger ones are located in southern states where vast tracts of land are cheap and the climate allows for year-round training. Fort Bragg near Fayetteville, North Carolina is 25 miles across and covers 129,000 acres, enough for artillery training. Fort Benning near Columbus, Georgia houses 95,000 trainees for a total population of 150,000. Large camps feature all the infrastructures and amenities of modern cities, including stores, movie theaters, barber and tailor shops, hospitals, banks, police forces, fire departments, telegraph and post offices, train stations, sewage systems, water works, public transportation, etc. Soldiers' barracks are usually one or two-story rectangular clapboard buildings constructed of rough lumber. Their unfinished interiors include dormitories with rows of steel-frame beds and bathrooms with sinks, showers and toilets. Hundreds of identical white-painted barracks arranged in gridded rows make it a challenge for new arrivals to orient themselves.

For most recruits, living far away from home among thousands of strangers from vastly different geographic and socio-economic backgrounds is intimidating. Many are shocked by the profanity that prevails in most camps. After taking the oath of enlistment, soldiers are stripped of almost every tangible connection to their civilian life or anything that distinguishes them as individuals. Their hair is shorn and they are compelled to mail their civilian clothing and personal possessions back home. For many, the complete loss of privacy is a jarring experience. Soldiers spend every second of the day and night in plain view of dozens, if not hundreds of other men. Public nudity becomes a fact of daily life, whether for embarrassing hygiene inspections, showers, changes of clothes, etc. Even toilets usually lack any sort of stalls or partitions.

These soldiers prepare their dormitory for inspection at Fort Belvoire, Virginia. U.S. Library of Congress photo.
The mobilization of millions of men creates an enormous marketing opportunity. Countless consumer goods are rebranded for the occasion, including this shoe polish kit (A), sewing kit (B) and button polishing cloth (C).

Trainees must quickly come to grip with a dizzying number of army rules. They have to learn to do everything from folding socks to firing rifles according to stringent army dictates, the transgression of which often carries disproportionate punishments. Paul Fussell wrote about one of his fellow trainees who, for having grabbed his sergeant's rifle by mistake, was made to wear his rifle slung diagonally across his body for a full week, including in bed, during meals and in the bathroom.[16]
Training requirements evolve through the war and also vary somewhat from camp to camp, depending on the style of the commanding officer and available amenities. By the end of the war, soldiers typically undergo thirteen weeks of basic training, followed by three or more weeks of specialization, depending on their assigned role. The following schedule from Camp Fannin, Texas[15] is representative of a typical day of basic training in 1944:

- 5:55, first call.
- 6:05, reveille; 15 minutes to wash up, get dressed and make beds.
- 6:20, march to the mess hall; 20 minutes for breakfast.
- 6:40, march back to barracks to prepare for the day's training activities.
- 8:00 to 5:30, training with a mid-day break for dinner.
- 5:30, march back to the barracks, then to the mess for supper.
- 7:00 to 9:15, housekeeping chores, study and free time.
- 9:15, preparation for bed.
- 9:45, taps, lights out.

Training courses include such subjects as military courtesy and discipline, close-order drill, first aid, chemical warfare, personal and sex hygiene, weapons training, mines and booby traps, map reading, close combat etc. The army makes abundant use of training films, some of which feature top Hollywood talent. Films are more engaging, they illustrate complex concepts with animations and storytelling, and they reduce the need for experienced instructors. Training courses alternate with physical conditioning in the form of calisthenics, marches, jogs and obstacle courses, sometimes carrying full loads of weapons and equipment. A typical obstacle course consists in crossing water-filled pits by jumping, with rope swings, over logs or monkey bars, crawling through tunnels or under barbwire entanglements, zigzagging through rows of posts, climbing palisades, etc. Marches become increasingly long and demanding, up to 36 miles - sometimes more - and double-time marches of 9 miles in two hours. Gradually, classroom instruction gives way to exercises designed to simulate increasingly realistic combat conditions, such as crawling under live machine gun fire, or attacking mock European villages. In addition to the daily training schedule, trainees are assigned night exercises, and various duties such as guard watches, or kitchen duty known as KP for Kitchen Patrol. In a letter to his sister dated May 10, 1942, John Duquoin writes: "I did a full day of KP duty, and it was exhausting. The damned thing lasted from 4:00 A.M. to 6:30 P.M. Since the kitchen at the induction center is an enormous one, with two large mess halls, we were kept rushing around like ants all day." Food is generally unsophisticated, but wholesome and plentiful. It provides about 4,300 calories per day, a necessary energy load for rigorous physical training.

Soldiers train six days per week and have precious little time to relax. In the evening, the PX is a favorite hangout where they can drink a few low-alcohol beers. Many prefer to retire to the relative quiet of their bunks to relax, read or write letters. On Sundays, unless they are assigned extra duty, or otherwise denied a pass, the men are usually allowed a few hours of free time to venture outside the camp and visit nearby towns.

If the first few days or weeks of basic training are a whirlwind of activity that leaves many frazzled and homesick, most soon feel at home in the regimented routine of Army life. They form friendships, break in their stiff uniforms and boots and transform into disciplined, healthy and confident soldiers. They also learn important unspoken rules of military life such as: Never volunteer for anything, do your best to blend in, and when addressed by an officer, maintain a nearly blank, but mildly concerned expression on your face. Bill Gast of the 743rd Tank Battalion concedes that he never mastered the all-important art of gold-bricking, which he defines as: "The ability to do as little as possible all day, but look frantically busy as soon as an officer enters the room."

Left: This friendly pamphlet welcomes new recruits to the reception center at Fort Sheridan near Chicago, Illinois. It includes a map and practical advice. Photo: These soldiers are climbing over the 8-foot palisade of the obstacle course at Camp Edwards, Massachusetts. U.S. Library of Congress photo.

Dress and Work Uniforms

Soldiers are forbidden to wear civilian clothing, even off-duty. On leave, they are to wear the dress uniform (A). Various badges and patches say a lot about the men wearing them. This particular uniform belonged to a Corporal of the first Infantry Division, as indicated by the two chevrons (B) and the famous "Big Red One" patch (C) on the shoulders. The round insignias on the collar (D) and the blue piping on the hat (E) are indicative of the infantry. The diagonal service bar on the sleeve (F) indicates that he has served three years in the military, including two and a half years overseas, six months for each horizontal bar (G). The "Ruptured Duck" patch (H) indicates that the soldier was honorably discharged.

Each soldier also receives a work uniform (I). Made of herringbone cotton twill for durability, it is intended for chores and messy work duties, but because of its comfortable cut and ruggedness, it became popular as a combat uniform.

Weapons Qualification

Naturally, the army places great emphasis on small arms training, something that soldiers generally find interesting and enjoyable. Training starts with classroom courses. In Fort Lewis, Washington on June 10, 1942, Don Mason writes: "We have been studying guns. Machine pistol, tomorrow rifles. […] I like to study the machine guns. There are about 100 pieces to memorize and identify. We have a test this Friday. Hope I make good." Training progresses to dry-firing, dummy ammunition drills, and finally to live fire on the weapons range. Rifles are fired from meticulously choreographed stances: Prone, kneeling, sitting and standing. Scorebooks (A) help soldiers keep track of their progress and include tables and diagrams to help adjust sights for distance and windage. A typical rifle range features a trench pit at one end to protect the target operators, and firing lines at distances of 1,000 inches, 200 yards, 300 yards and sometimes 500 yards. During slow fire exercises, target operators lower large paper targets after each shot to locate the bullet hole and repair it with a sticker. The target is then raised and a black disk on a pole is placed over the impact point to make it visible to the shooter. If the target is missed entirely, the spotter waves a small red flag colloquially known as "Maggie's drawers" in reference to a bawdy song titled "Those old red flannel drawers that Maggie wore." On August 1, 1942, Don Mason writes: "On the rifle range I shot 119 out of a possible 150. I didn't do so good standing up. I didn't get a "Maggie's drawers". We shot lying down, sitting up, kneeling, standing, standing and dropping to kneeling, standing and dropping to lying down – 5 shots in each position. I shot 3 bull's eyes at 200 yards lying down – in an eight inch circle." At the end of weapons training, each soldier must pass a qualification shooting course. According to his score, he receives a badge (B) with a rating of marksman, sharpshooter or expert.

Sergeant George Camblair is trained at Fort Belvoir, Virginia in September 1942. U.S. Library of Congress photo.

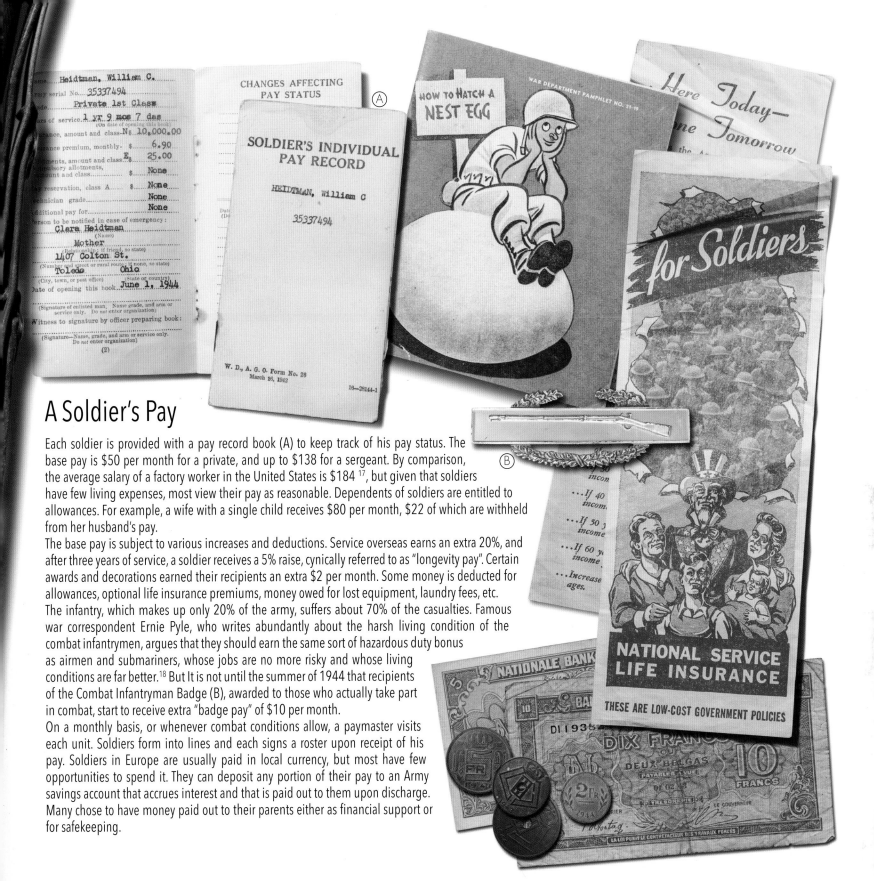

A Soldier's Pay

Each soldier is provided with a pay record book (A) to keep track of his pay status. The base pay is $50 per month for a private, and up to $138 for a sergeant. By comparison, the average salary of a factory worker in the United States is $184 [17], but given that soldiers have few living expenses, most view their pay as reasonable. Dependents of soldiers are entitled to allowances. For example, a wife with a single child receives $80 per month, $22 of which are withheld from her husband's pay.

The base pay is subject to various increases and deductions. Service overseas earns an extra 20%, and after three years of service, a soldier receives a 5% raise, cynically referred to as "longevity pay". Certain awards and decorations earned their recipients an extra $2 per month. Some money is deducted for allowances, optional life insurance premiums, money owed for lost equipment, laundry fees, etc.

The infantry, which makes up only 20% of the army, suffers about 70% of the casualties. Famous war correspondent Ernie Pyle, who writes abundantly about the harsh living condition of the combat infantrymen, argues that they should earn the same sort of hazardous duty bonus as airmen and submariners, whose jobs are no more risky and whose living conditions are far better.[18] But It is not until the summer of 1944 that recipients of the Combat Infantryman Badge (B), awarded to those who actually take part in combat, start to receive extra "badge pay" of $10 per month.

On a monthly basis, or whenever combat conditions allow, a paymaster visits each unit. Soldiers form into lines and each signs a roster upon receipt of his pay. Soldiers in Europe are usually paid in local currency, but most have few opportunities to spend it. They can deposit any portion of their pay to an Army savings account that accrues interest and that is paid out to them upon discharge. Many chose to have money paid out to their parents either as financial support or for safekeeping.

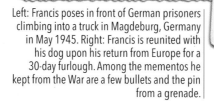

"Fran" Gaudere joins the army on April Fool's day of 1943. He is assigned to the 119th Infantry Regiment, a component of the highly distinguished 30th Infantry Division nicknamed the "Roosevelt's SS" by German soldiers. He receives basic training at Camp Blanding, Florida before his division is sent to Camp Joseph T. Robinson in Little Rock, Arkansas where Fran is trained as a radio operator. On June 4th 1943, Fran and about 5,000 other men set off across the Atlantic from Boston, Massachusetts on an unescorted ocean liner. Fran recalls: "They said that the ship was so fast that the subs couldn't catch us. But what if they were waiting ahead of us?" Fran spends a year in England training for the invasion of France. He lands on Omaha Beach six days after D-day and catches up with his outfit near St. Lo. Fran remembers: "From the day we got to France to the day we won, we were in the war all the way. We didn't have any passes for leaves or anything. We were constantly fighting the Germans. We never saw our duffle bags until after the war." Fran carries an M1 Garand Rifle and a 44-pound SRC-284 radio. His job consists in making himself available to officers

Left: Francis poses in front of German prisoners climbing into a truck in Magdeburg, Germany in May 1945. Right: Francis is reunited with his dog upon his return from Europe for a 30-day furlough. Among the mementos he kept from the War are a few bullets and the pin from a grenade.

for communication with other Companies or Battalions: "I'd call back ammunition, or litter carriers and stuff like that." Of the nine Radio Operators in his platoon, six die in Europe.

Following the German counter-offensive at Mortain, he witnesses what would remain his most haunting memory of the war: "Our trucks were on a hill, and there were some dead Germans there and it was hot. They were all bloated and they had maggots in their eyes and their mouths. I can still see them every once in a while. Of course I have seen a lot of guys getting shot and die, and even frozen, but that was the worst."

Because he is usually very close to the front lines, Fran has little contact with civilians. He recalls: "Either the Germans kicked them out of the towns or if there was anybody left, it was a few that were hiding in the cellars. They weren't too friendly because we were destroying their buildings."

Right before the Battle of the Bulge, having reached the Roer river east of Aachen, Germany, Fran's 119th Regiment pulls back for refitting and rest. On December 17, a day after the start of the offensive, the 30th Infantry Division is rushed south to counter Kampfgruppe Peiper's thrust along the Amblève river. Fran remembers: "Our whole division was transported past Liège, down to around Stoumont. And that was a cold trip in open trucks. We were half frozen by the time we got there. [...] Gradually my feet got colder and colder. We wore regular combat boots, no galoshes. We had no winter clothes. Of course your feet would get wet and we'd take the socks off and put them on our belts. The heat of our bodies dried the socks off and we'd keep swapping." When they can, the men find refuge in buildings: "They had what they called briquettes: Black bricks of coal dust or something. We all carried a few of those with us so we could light them up and try and keep warm after we got inside some place. We had one thin blanket. And the sleeping bags, they weren't puffy. It was just a thin piece of cloth in there. They really didn't keep you warm." Fran remembers attending Christmas Mass in a bombed out church in La Gleize.

Riflemen from an armored division are marching south-east of Born on January 22, 1945. U.S. National Archives.

M3 "Grease Gun"

The M3 submachine gun is introduced to front line service late in 1944 as the successor of the Thompson (See page 51). Its design is inspired by the minimalism of the British Sten gun. To simplify manufacturing, the barrel and bolt are the only parts that are precision-machined. The rest of the gun is made mostly of stamped sheet metal parts welded or riveted together. The result has a some-what toy-like appearance that GIs liken to a me-chanic's grease gun. Ralph Schip of the 18th Cavalry Reconnaissance Squadron, the proud owner of a Thompson submachine gun derides M3s as: "Those crazy grease-gun plumbers' friends.[19]" Nonetheless the M3 establishes itself as rugged and dependable. It is substantially lighter and more compact than the Thompson, and costs only half as much. The M3 is so affordable that it is viewed almost as a disposable weapon and Army Armorers do not stock spare parts for it. The relatively slow rate of fire of the M3 (about 400 rounds per minute) makes for steadier aim and saves ammunition.

The ejection port cover (A) doubles as a safety; when closed, it renders the gun inoperable. While the M3 fires only in full-automatic mode, one can squeeze out single shots with quick releases of the trigger. The removable, telescopic shoulder stock can be used as a cleaning rod. It can also serve as a wrench to unscrew the gun barrel and features a steel tab (B) to help reload the 30-round magazine. Notice the small oiler tube (C) on the left side and the way two magazines have been taped together head-to-toe (D) for quick reloading.

The Arsenal of Democracy

If the vast majority of American civilians never experience the brutality of the war first-hand, they nonetheless play a crucial role in its outcome. Ultimately, Germany would not be defeated by superior skill, bravery or tactics, it would be defeated by the seemingly limitless flow of weapons, airplanes, fuel and ammunition from America's extraordinary industrial capacity. As President Roosevelt has vowed in a famous radio speech, America has indeed become the "arsenal of democracy".

Through much of 1941, the average American is little concerned with the distant turmoil in Europe and in the Pacific. America backs the Allies with food and war supplies through the Lend Lease act, but public opinion is resolutely opposed to direct military intervention. All that changes on the morning of December 7th, 1941 with the Japanese bombing of Pearl Harbor. The shock and outrage of the attack soon turns into a yearning for revenge. Americans become fully and zealously committed to the War effort. Hundreds of thousands of young men volunteer for service. Military planners estimate that a war on two vast and distant fronts will require the mobilization of some 8.8 million men.[13] Training and equipping such a formidable force will require several years and the full backing of America's industrial resources. A month after the attack on Pearl Harbor, President Roosevelt sets startlingly ambitious military production goals for the next two years: One million machine guns, 185,000 airplanes, 120,000 tanks, 55,000 antiaircraft guns and 18 million deadweight tons of merchant shipping.[20] Thousands of military barracks are constructed in military camps throughout the United States and billions of dollars' worth of military contracts are issued for everything from army shoelaces to aircraft carriers.

Eager to cash in, factories everywhere convert to war production. Automobile plants retool for tanks and aircrafts production, toys and appliance companies switch to grenades, bullets, or small arms manufacture. Factories introduce swing shifts to extend their operation to 24 hours a day, seven days a week. Workers from rural communities flock to cities where well-paid defense jobs are plentiful. To make up for the millions of young men serving in the military, women are encouraged to suspend their traditional role as homemakers by trading their aprons for coveralls and welding goggles. Natural resources and food production are diverted to the war effort, resulting in shortages of consumer goods. New cars, refrigerators or radios become nearly impossible to find. The newly formed Office for Price Administration imposes rationing on most consumer goods, including gasoline, tires, and foodstuff. Soon, "Victory" recipe books propose cake without eggs, or apple pies without apples. In 1943, the peak production year, some 20 million private "Victory" vegetable gardens produce 40% of the vegetables consumed in America.[21]

The war is financed in good part through the sale of War Bonds in denominations ranging from $25 (about two weeks of the average salary) to $10,000. War Bonds sell at 75% of their face value and mature in ten years. Children and small investors save towards War Bonds by collecting War Stamps. Boosted by patriotism, advertising campaigns and the endorsement of the era's biggest movie and music stars, the sale of War bonds and stamps exceeds all expectations.

Civil organizations too are eager

to perform their patriotic duty. The American Red Cross organizes blood drives, clothing collections and knitting clubs for war relief. Boy scouts gather scrap metal, paper and tires for the war effort. School children are challenged to form as large a ball as possible with the tin foil from gum wrappers and cigarette packs before turning it in for scrap. Housewives are asked to save tin cans and waste kitchen fat to be recycled into ammunition and explosives. Futile as some of these scrap collections are, they give everyone a token opportunity to show support for the war effort.

Advertisers and marketers fuel the surge in patriotism and exploit it with liberal use of popular slogans such as "Remember Pearl Harbor", "Buy War Bonds" or "Keep'em Flying" and by suggesting that buying their product will somehow hasten victory. Brands are redesigned in red, white and blue or with smiling soldiers, sailors and marines. One can purchase special "Victory" hairpins or "Victory" fly swatters that conserve metal for the war. Through its *Lucky Strike green goes to war!* campaign, the famous brand of cigarettes switches its packaging from green to white, supposedly to save pigment for the army's olive drab.

Naturally, the war dominates newspapers, radio programs and movie theater newsreels. People are intently following the progress of American boys on special "Victory" maps sponsored by national brands.

The war effort permeates every aspect of day-to-day life. Never before have Americans of all creeds been so tightly united behind a singular purpose. In spite of the privations, anxiety and the heartache caused by the departure and the death of so many young men, many Americans would go on to remember the war years with nostalgia. Herb Adams of the 82nd Airborne Division recalls that for the people at home, the war was like the biggest football game in history: "The whole country was cheering for the same team, and everybody had a friend or relative in the game."

These two women (A) work on the wing of a bomber at the Douglas Aircraft Company. Employee badges (B) are a security measure brought about by the fear of industrial spies and saboteurs. Every American is issued books of rationing coupons for food (C). Red coupons are required for meat or dairy products, blue coupons for other types of processed food. Cardboard tokens are given as change. This window sticker (D) is intended to fight black market activity by appealing to women's sense of decency and civic pride. Purchasers of War Bonds can display their patriotism with window stickers like this one (E). These "Victory" hairpins (F) claim to be made with less steel to conserve for the war effort.

Left : Charles Preston cleans his frozen machine gun on December 21, 1944. Above : A road block manned by the 45th Infantry Division. U.S. Army photos.

.30 Browning Machine Gun

The M1917 Browning machine gun (A) arrives too late to see significant action in World War I, but with minor upgrades and alongside its M1919 air-cooled version (B), it establishes itself as a dependable machine gun during World War II. The M1917 and M1919 are recoil-operated machine guns. With each shot, a short recoil in the barrel imparts enough momentum to the bolt to actuate the reloading cycle. Ammunition is fed from cotton belts of 250 rounds of .30-06 Springfield cartridges, the same round fired by the M1 Garand and the BAR. The M1917 with its bulky water sleeve and tripod weighs close to 100 pounds without ammunition and requires a crew of four men to be deployed, hence it is mostly used in static roles or mounted on vehicles. The water jacket proves problematic in the intense cold of the Ardennes. Wesley Ross of the 146th Engineer Combat Battalion recalls: "One of our water-cooled Brownings fired one round only and then sat there mute. The water in the cooling jacket had frozen, jamming the action!4" The M1919 only weighs half as much as the M1917, but if not fired sparingly, it can overheat to the point of failure. When a gunner releases the trigger to stop firing, the next round sits fully chambered in the barrel. If the barrel is too hot it can set off the round unexpectedly. To avoid this dangerous situation known as a cook-off, gunners are trained to eject the last round when they are done firing. Veteran tank driver Bill Gast of the 30th Infantry Division remembers the horrifying death of a fellow soldier who, during a break in an intense battle, walked up to the front of a Sherman tank to talk with its commander in the turret. The assistant driver's M1919 machine gun cooked off a round that nearly cut the soldier in half.

Herb Adams was a machine gunner in the 504th Parachute Infantry Division. He carried the M1919A6 version with a bipod and a shoulder stock. He remembers: "In the Battle of the Bulge it was cold, sometimes it was soaking wet, you've got rain, then it freezes and the damned thing never let me down. You didn't want to put your bare hand on the machine gun. When you used up the ammunition, you keep the belt. You use that belt to wrap around where your hand would go, otherwise your hand would actually freeze to that gun."

The Robots Attack

The city of Liège, situated to the northwest of the Ardennes at the confluent of the Meuse and the Ourthe Rivers, is the largest and most important city in the region. It is a pivotal railway hub, and along with adjacent towns, it forms one of Europe's great industrial centers. On September 7 and 8, 1944, Liège is liberated by elements of the 3rd Tank Battalion. The city quickly becomes a key logistical center for the American push into Germany. The Sart-Tilman, Monsin and Droixhe Island neighborhoods soon become the sites of colossal supply depots, and four General Hospitals are established in and around the city. But as the inhabitants celebrate the arrival of their American liberators, little do they know that the worst of their suffering is yet to come.

From the end of September 1944 to the end of January 1945, the city is attacked by waves of Nazi V weapons. The V stands for *Vergeltungswaffen* (Vengeance weapons). First come the V2s, the world's first long-range ballistic missiles. The V2 is the result of Werner Von Braun's pioneering work in liquid-fueled rocket technology. The 45-foot, 13-ton V2, carries a payload of a ton of high explosive. Because it falls to earth at several times the speed of sound, it cannot be heard as it approaches and it is immune to air defense systems. In three weeks, twenty-seven V2 rockets explode in and around Liège. This first wave is only the prelude to even more violent attacks with less technologically advanced, but more numerous V1 flying bombs that locals nickname "robots". The V1 is a small pilotless airplane nicknamed "buzz bomb" by Americans because of the distinctive rumbling sound of its pulse jet engine. It is launched from a catapult or dropped from a plane and guided by autopilot on a set course. A vane-driven odometer counts down the distance to the target, then triggers a mechanism that forces the V1 into a steep dive. Incidentally, this sudden maneuver interrupts the flow of gasoline, thus shutting down the loud engine and giving the people below a terrifying notice that the V1 with its 1,800 pounds of high-explosives is about to strike.

William Campbell of the 28th Division remembers milling about with hundreds of other soldiers on the large town square of a Belgian city (likely Liège). Everybody has an ear attuned to the rumbling of a V1 flying overhead. The sound suddenly stops and everybody runs for shelter. What strikes Bill at that moment is the crescendo of hundreds of army boots on the cobblestones: "It sounded like you were at the opera and everybody started to applaud. We heard the V1 explode maybe seven or eight blocks away."

Veteran Alphonse G. York of the 309th Engineer Combat Battalion recalls watching V1s from a hill overlooking the city: "We'd see the big explosion and we'd hear the noise. So we figured every second is one mile so we would be able to judge that we were roughly 3 or 4 miles away."

Frank Maresca of the 75th Infantry Division remembers sitting in a train stopped in a rail yard in Liège one night. Another soldier who had been a coal miner points out that the "Gondola-type" boxcar next to theirs is the type that transports dynamite. Right around that time, they hear an approaching sound that Frank compares to that of a car without a muffler. He wrote: "That buzz bomb went the entire length of the boxcars, then it went dead. That was followed by an uncanny silence […] Then it came! The flying bomb with its one-ton warhead hit something several hundred yards in front and to the right of our route back towards the Huy area. The roar and concussion were tremendous! The light created by the blast was equivalent to the brightness of a clear day at high noon. The entire train of boxcars shook from one end to the other, first bumping into one another and then rocking from side to side.[22]"

Marie Davis works for the Red Cross at the 16th Field Hospital in Jupille, a suburb of Liége. The hospital itself would be hit by three V1s. In a letter to her family and friends, she recounts patients rushing outside at the sound of the air-raid sirens to catch a glimpse of "ugly gray sharks of the air with flames spitting from their tails." She relates their terrible toll: "Each day as we were commuting back and forth from our hospital, we passed fresh evidence of devastation, and more blocks where house after house was leveled. Once, the street was blocked for half an hour while debris was shoveled from the highway so we could proceed, and they were still digging for bodies."

The men fighting in the Ardennes watch the V1 streaking westwards across the sky. At the beginning of the offensive, they boost the morale of German soldiers as they lend credence to the Nazi propaganda predicting that advanced secret weapons would turn the tide of the war.

The relentless bombings take a heavy psychological toll on the inhabitants of Liège. First comes the sound of the massive air-raid sirens distributed throughout the city. Their ebbing and flowing overlaps into a sinister wail that sends even cats scurrying for basements. Those without basements seek refuge with neighbors, in public shelters or crawl under tables. Front doors are left unlocked to permit passersby to find shelter. Passages have been cut through walls separating adjacent basements to allow escape routes in case of collapses. With bated breath, people strain to hear the approaching rumble of the robot, speculating as to its direction and distance. Marie-Thérèse Hanot, a citizen of Liège wrote: "Ah! This short moment of silence when the V1 stopped! It was a great suspense. It seemed like our heart stopped as well. And what a relief when we heard it explode like thunder. We had dodged another bullet![23]" Walls tremble, windows shatter, lights flicker and there is a smell of plaster in the air. Finally, the air-raid sirens erupt in a long, continuous wail to sound the all-clear. And this nightmarish game of Russian roulette is repeated over and over again. Ms Hanot counts as many as thirty V1 in a single day.[23] At times, procuring food becomes nearly impossible as intervals between air raids are too short to stand in long grocery lines. Marie Davis notes in her letter that about December 11, in the days leading up to the Battle of the Bulge, the attacks intensify after a brief respite: "Liège, a beautiful city of 200,000 became a shambles of its former self. Each new trip to town brought to light more destruction. Shops

that we had patronized were gone. A flower shop that had donated fifty plants to our hospital a week before was a shell, when I went past it. The center of town was hit, the cathedral badly damaged, the arcade where we had done most of our shopping left without a single window in the stores."

Lieutenant Dorothy Barre, a nurse in the same hospital remembers: "When you get done at the end of a work shift, you're so

tired, and because of those damn buzz bombs coming every night, you know, they wake you up. They'd start around 11:00. And you try to get some sleep to get back on duty." As the attacks become more frequent, sleep-deprived civilians take to sleeping in their basements. Georgette Mernier, who is six years old at the time, lives in an apartment in Seraing, a suburb of Liége. She recalls sleeping in a small basement: "The whole family was piled up. We had brought mattresses down from the bedrooms. I had three brothers and sisters, plus my mom, her sister-in-law and my cousin."

It is tempting to believe that the V1 is devilishly accurate when it strikes or barely misses important buildings such as a school, hospital or factory, but in reality, due to its rudimentary guidance system, the V1 cannot be aimed at anything smaller than large urban areas. Maps of impact sites reveal a random pattern that extends as far as 7 miles from the center of the Liège. Marcel Schmetz recalls playing around the wreckage of a V1 that crash-landed without exploding in his hometown of Clermont, 12 miles short of Liège.

The robots cannot serve any strategic purpose. True to their name, they prove nothing more than the vindictive act of a hateful and desperate ideology.

According to historian Lambert Graillet, 2,141 V1s hit Liége and nearby towns. Liège, with 5.7 hits per square kilometer is more severely struck than either London or Antwerp who respectively received 1.5 and 4.2 hits per square kilometer. In Liège alone, 2,407 people die, many thousands more are wounded and some 20,588 houses are either severely damaged or destroyed. Yet nobody

suffers more from the V1 and V2 than the slave laborers who build them. They are drawn from concentration camps and subsist for a while in underground factories without heat or sanitation and with little food or light. When their horrific work conditions, diseases and starvation lead to manufacturing defects, they are accused of sabotage and many are brutally tortured and killed. Some are hung from the cranes directly over the production lines to die slow, suffocating deaths in plain view of their fellow workers, where their bodies are then left hanging for days.[25]

Ougrée, Belgium, January 12, 1945. These civilians have been living in a basement since the destruction of their house by a V1 in November. U.S. National Archives.

US Rifle, Cal .30, M1 "Garand"

The US Rifle, Cal .30, M1 is better known by the last name of its inventor, French-Canadian-born Jean Cantius Garand. The rifle is the first standard-issue semi-automatic rifle in the world. Prior to the Second World War, developing semi-automatic military rifles is controversial. Many among the military leadership believe that semi-automatic rifles are too complicated, costly and unreliable and that rapid fire will lead soldiers to waste ammunition.
The Garand is gas-operated. This means that some of the high-pressure gas from each cartridge is diverted to a piston that actuates the automatic reloading mechanism. The Garand is loaded with internal "en-bloc" clips that hold eight rounds each (A). After all eight rounds have been fired, the clip automatically ejects, and the breech remains open and ready to accept a new clip. The sight of the Garand features a knob on each side. One adjusts the sight laterally for windage, the other vertically for range. A compartment drilled into the stock contains a cleaning kit (B) that includes grease and oil. The M1 proves accurate and dependable and is well liked by the soldiers. General George Patton hails it as "The greatest battle implement ever devised."

Franck Vukasin of the 83rd Division pauses to reload his rifle near Houffalize on January 15, 1945.
U.S. Army photo

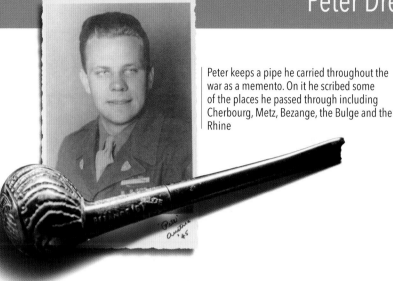

Peter keeps a pipe he carried throughout the war as a memento. On it he scribed some of the places he passed through including Cherbourg, Metz, Bezange, the Bulge and the Rhine

Peter Drevinski grows up in Middleborough, Massachusetts. After graduating from High School in 1943, he qualifies for the Army Specialized Training Program that prepares academically gifted young men for Army jobs requiring advance scientific or technical skills. Following a thirteen-week basic military training, Peter is sent to the University of Maine in Orono to pursue an accelerated engineering degree. "It turned out that Patton needed some help from the infantry to back up his tanks", recalls Peter, "so the program was phased out. I was taken out of the college dormitory and transferred down to Tennessee to join the 26th Yankee Division." Peter is trained as a BAR gunner. He participates in large-scale maneuvers and is sent to Fort Jackson, South Carolina for further training. In August 1944, he embarks for Cherbourg, France. He recalls: "It took ten or eleven days to cross the Atlantic, and half that time to overcome seasickness."

Peter mostly walks across France, carrying his heavy BAR. The Yankee Division first sees action near the Saar River, fighting its way to the Maginot Line along the German border. About that time, Peter's feet give out. After a brief hospitalization, he is reassigned as a runner, which, as Peter wryly points out: "is certainly not consistent with the problem with my feet." He is transferred to another unit against his protest. He explains: "During basic training, you build a very strong bond between the men. When I was told that I had to transfer to another unit, I objected, I didn't want to go."

As a runner, Peter's role consists in hand-delivering messages when they cannot be communicated safely by telephone or radio. As a security measure, he often has to transmit verbal messages as well, without which the written messages he carries do not make sense or cannot be authenticated. He is part of a pool of runners on standby near the command post, ready to head out at a moment's notice. The task is often challenging and dangerous. Peter has to find his way over unfamiliar territory alone without a map, sometimes in the chaos of battle. He recalls: "You had some high points that were pointed out to you, there were areas that you should avoid, but are you looking at the right landmark? Are you in the right place? If they call for artillery fire, are you gonna be in the middle of it? Traveling at night, in a city you don't know or in the woods, all the sudden you hear: "Jawohl Johann! Was gibst?" and you lay flat and still for what seems like hours before you leave." A white cape and hood help Peter blend in with the deep snow of the Ardennes, but he recalls that crossing rivers is often challenging: "There were times when I got to my knees in water just above freezing, and you still have to continue […] That was a hazard at the Bulge particularly. It was very cold and when the rivers are strong in their flow, they don't freeze and you have to watch where you are going. You can't take a half hour to look around, you gotta go otherwise you're a standing target."

Among the dark memories of the Battle of the Bulge, a bright spot stands out in the form of an unexpected Christmas meal in a hamlet somewhere in the Ardennes, the first hot food Peter had in a long time: "It was poultry of some kind. I ate it as if it were turkey. Heaven forbid, we're in the middle of a battle and we get a Christmas meal! If I recall, we even got cranberry sauce. You can bet your bottom dollar, the morale really improved."

M1918A2 Browning Automatic Rifle (BAR)

At the time of its introduction late in World War I, the BAR is an innovative weapon, designed to be fired from the hip while advancing. By World War II, it is outclassed by other machine guns such as the British Bren, but having failed to develop a better alternative for light automatic fire squad support, and with a sizable stock on hand, the US Army carries the BAR over with only minor upgrades. These include the addition of a hinged butt plate (A) to help support the weight over the shoulder, a magazine guide (B) to make the insertion of magazines easier, and a damper mechanism located in the stock to give the gunner the option of reducing the rate of fire from 550 rounds per minutes down to about 350. In 1942, a Bakelite stock (C) is introduced in response to shortages of high-grade walnut lumber.

A typical twelve-men rifle squad includes one BAR gunner. The BAR gunner plays a key role in the classic fire and maneuver tactic. He is tasked with laying a base of fire to keep the enemy pinned down while riflemen seek flanking approaches or more advantageous lines of fire.

The BAR fires the standard Springfield .30-06 cartridge from twenty-round magazines (D). The small capacity of the magazines is a major shortcoming, but larger magazine would impede the rifle's operation in the prone position. A twenty-round magazine is only sufficient for four or five short bursts, which means that BAR gunners spend more time reloading than firing. Furthermore, they have to pace their fire to avoid overheating the thin-walled barrel. A sustainable rate of fire is limited to around 80 rounds per minute. A loaded BAR weights about 21 pounds, more than twice the weight of a Garand Rifle. A full complement of ammunition brings the total load to around 40 pounds. Many gunners discard the poorly designed bipod (E) and the flash guard (F) to save weight.

Personal Belongings

Soldiers carry very little in the way of personal items, but these few objects and documents take on very high sentimental value; they are a tenuous link with the civilian lives they had to set aside and among the few possessions that distinguish them as individuals. Soldiers' wallets typically hold assortments of currencies they have picked up along the way, personal documents and photos of loved ones. Having no way of locking away money or valuables, many soldiers wear money belts (A) around their waste under their clothes. Watches are a classic high school graduation gift. John McAuliffe of the 87th Infantry Division recalls that his was the only watch in his squad and that it was passed from man to man on guard duty.

Many soldiers turn to religion to seek courage and solace. They carry religious medals (B) offered to them by parents or friends as good luck charms. American churches, synagogues and religious organizations publish all sorts of miniature prayer books specifically for soldiers. The Stuart Bible Company sells a "Protecto shield" New Testament (C). It comes in a metallic shell that, when placed in the breast pocket, is supposed to shield the soldier's heart from bullets.

Get Up You Son of a Bitch!

Herb Adams of the 82nd Airborne Division mans a machine gun position on the edge of a forest near the Siegfried line. His Company has repulsed an attack earlier that evening. German corpses, plainly visible in the moonlight, are scattered in the snowy field ahead of him. Pistol in hand and accompanied by his friend Lester, Herb ventures out to search the bodies for souvenirs. Herb remembers: "I told my buddies on the machine gun: 'Don't chew us up on the way back in.' There were bodies all over the place. I don't know what possessed me but I gave one of them a kick and said: 'Get up you son of a bitch!' The next thing I know, three Germans were standing up with their hands in the air! One of the guys started speaking in perfect English. Now I'm really confused! What the hell is this?"

In the conversation that ensues, Herb finds out that the English-speaking German has a twin brother serving in Herb's regiment. The twins grew up in Chicago with parents who have emigrated from Germany. Right before the war, one of the twins and his father had traveled to Germany to visit relatives while the other twin and his mother stayed home in the United States. When Hitler declared war on the United States, the father and son became trapped in Germany, and because they are considered German citizens, they were forced into the Wehrmacht. Herb remembers: "How

the mail got from one to the other, I don't know, but they corresponded during the war and each clearly knew where the other was." The soldier further explains that there are about one hundred men left in his unit. They have nothing to eat and are simply trying to retake a food cache hidden under the snow. Herb suggests that the three men go back and tell their unit that if they all surrender the next morning, they will get all the food they want. Lester and Herb return to their line and report to an infuriated Lieutenant: "We told him what we had done and that there was going to be a flashlight signal tomorrow at six o'clock in the morning, and the signal was gonna mean that they were going to surrender, so don't fire at them. He was definitely going to court-martial me because if you get prisoners, you don't turn them loose. You bring them in, and you let somebody else interrogate them, then if they want to send them back to surrender that's one thing. But some damned private doesn't do that!"

Herb did not sleep at all that night. The next morning at 6:00, flashlights signal up and down the line and about one hundred German soldier walk out in the open with their hands in the air. As Herb and his fellow paratroopers round up the prisoners, he asks his Lieutenant: "When do I get my medal?" The lieutenant replies: "We're even now!" The twin brother of the German prisoner is later assigned to the detachment that escorts the prisoners to the rear. Thus the twin brothers are reunited for the first time in three years.

Paratroopers of the 82nd Airborne Division man a machine gun in Odrimont on January 6, 1945. They have "freed" a door to cover their foxhole and keep a grenade within quick reach. U.S. National Archives.

Light Tank M5 "Stuart"

Less weight makes for a faster, more maneuverable tank that can better keep up with wheeled vehicles. Light tanks can pass over secondary bridges and handle difficult terrain that would bar heavier tanks. The Stuart tank M3 is introduced in 1941 and sees several modifications and upgrades before it is superseded by the M24 Chaffee at the end of the war (See page 82) The M5 shown here represents a major upgrade introduced in 1942. The most significant modification is the substitution of the radial engine - in high demand for airplane manufacture - with twin V8 Cadillac car engines. The M5 is renown for its mechanical reliability and proudly nicknamed the "Cadillac tank" by its crews. It also features a roomier welded hull with a sloped glacis front plate that gives it the appearance of a scaled-down Sherman tank. The trade-offs for the Stuart's agility and speed are a thin armor and a weak 37mm main gun. By 1944, the Stuart has already become obsolete as it stands no chance against German panzers and anti-tank weapons. It is primarily used for reconnaissance missions, for infantry fire support or for escort duties. The Stuart is generally crewed by four men: A commander, a gunner, a driver and an assistant driver. It can reach a top speed of about 36 mph and a range of about 100 miles. In addition to its main 37mm gun, the Stuart sports three .30 Browning machine guns: one coaxial with the main gun, one operated from the right bow by the assistant driver and one mounted on top of the turret.

An M5 Stuart of the 3rd Armored Division surveys the sky on December 18, 1944. U.S. Army photo.

Christian and Jeanne de Marcken Remember

Left photo: Mrs. de Marcken had this photo taken in 1942 to send to her husband who was in Germany at the Lauffen prisoner of war camp. In the back row from left to right: Myriam, with brother Louis in front of her, Mrs. Alix de Marcken, Butch, Christian and Françoise. In the front row: Pierre, Jacqueline, Béatrice and Anne. Right photo: Christian's father Gustave de Marcken upon his return from the prisoner camp.

Christian de Marcken is twelve years old when Hitler invades Belgium in May of 1940. He is the eldest of eight siblings - soon to be nine - born in Belgium of an American businessman and a Belgian mother. The family rents a castle in Bierges, Belgium. Because the very large property is located on a defensive line built early in the war, it encompasses eighteen concrete pillboxes and numerous steel anti-tank structures known as "Belgian gates" (The Germans would later relocate these barriers to the Normandy coast as part of their "Atlantic Wall".) In their attempt to halt the German advance, British expeditionary forces establish a battery of enormous 16" guns on the de Marckens' lawn. Christian recalls: "When these guns were fired you had the impression the roof of our home was going up and dropping back down." Christian also vividly recalls the presence of African men of the 11th French Zouave Infantry who went about barefoot and collected the ears of the Germans they had killed to hang them on strings around their necks.

Eventually, the family is forced to flee their home. They attempt to reach southern France in the hope of escaping to America, but the Germans catch up with them in Azy-le-Vif, only fourteen miles from free France. The family heads back to Belgium only to find that their home has been taken over by a Luftwaffe motor-pool. Christian remembers an arrogant German lieutenant standing at the doorstep shouting: "America a small country, Germany a big country. Raus!" Because America is still neutral at the time, the US Embassy obtains from the Germans that they vacate the house, but not before they

plug all the toilets, defecate in all the beds, urinate everywhere and steal or destroy an estimated $52,000 worth of antiques and furniture (worth close to a million dollars in today's money).

The situation goes from bad to worse on December 11, 1941 when Hitler declares war on the United States. Christian's father is arrested as an enemy national and sent to a prisoner of war camp in Germany. Even after his father's deportation, the Germans remain suspicious of the family and a German guard is permanently posted in their house. On several occasions, SS troops storm the house in the middle of the night. They search every room and gather everybody at gunpoint, then make sure that the number of warm beds accounts for everybody, lest the family is hiding someone. Somehow the Germans never realize that there is one child too many in the family, a young Jewish boy Mrs. de Marcken has taken in.

For a single mother with ten young children and no financial support, life soon becomes a struggle. Christian recalls that the so-called flour the Germans make available is mostly sugar beet pulp, the residue of sugar production ordinarily fed to livestock: "It would not rise, it made brownish black bread. The knife got stuck and covered with a glue-like brown sticky stuff." To supplement the very strict rationing, the family grows vegetables and a little wheat. The children raise a few geese, chickens, rabbits, a goat for milk, and at one time hide a pig in the woods. Being the eldest boy in the family, Christian has the unenviable task of killing the rabbits and skinning them. He also becomes adept at trapping hare and pigeons with snares. In their haste to vacate the house, British and German troops have left behind ammunition and explosives that prove irresistible to a twelve-year-old boy. Christian recalls improvising pipe cannons with spaghetti-like cordite explosive to entertain his siblings, and detonating German "potato masher" grenades for fun behind a tall stone wall in the garden. "How we all came out alive from these war years is a miracle" marvels Christian.

The very harsh conditions of the prisoner of war camp take a severe toll on Christian's father. He is released after two and a half years, only because the Nazis believe that his death from kidney failure is imminent. Upon his return to Belgium, he is so emaciated that Mrs. de Marcken and the children do not recognize him at first. In 1944, Mr. de Marcken is denounced for assisting a downed allied aviator and arrested once again by the Nazis. He is to be executed by firing squad on September 13, 1944, but as the Allies close in, the Nazis attempt to evacuate prisoners to Germany. His train is stopped by Allied ground-attack fighters and he is among more than 1,500 prisoners who manage to escape.

On August 18, 1944, fourteen-years-old Jeanne and her sister Marguerite take the tramway from Avin to Wierde to visit an older sister. They have reached an overpass in the city of Namur when the air raid sirens comes on and the tramway stops. From their precarious vantage point, the two sisters witness a flight of American B17 bombers drop their payload and the center of the city erupts in fire, dust and smoke. As it turns out, the bombers have missed their target, which happens to be the bridge upon which Jeanne and her sister are standing. Some 330 civilians die

and close to 2,000 buildings are destroyed or damaged in the bombing.

A few weeks later, Jeanne's father hears from a local farmer that the Americans are approaching. In spite of the late hour and the darkness, the overjoyed daughters manage to convince their father to go meet their American liberators. The party is walking towards Burdinne when it finds itself in the middle of a firefight with Americans on one side, Germans on the other and farm buildings and haystacks burning on both sides. The terrified group hides in a ditch along a hedgerow. Jeanne remembers that with them in the ditch are several dead Germans and a Belgian man trying to pull the boots off one of the bodies. Christian and Jeanne would eventually meet after the war. They marry and move to the United states in 1955.

Christian and Jeanne de Marcken are holding the flag that Christian's mother secretly sewed together at night while their German guard was asleep, and kept hidden under a floorboard until the day of liberation. Not entirely familiar with the details of the flag, she sewed the stars upside down.

Short-Term Prisoners

Around January 15, 1945, somewhere on a hill between the towns of Ennal and Spineux, men from the 106th Infantry Division enjoy a respite from the fighting. Chuck Wenc (See page 131) and his machine gun crew are ordered to take position down in the valley below. The three men walk down and start to dig a T-shaped machine gun emplacement. Digging through the frozen soil is strenuous work. The men soon take a break, sit down and light cigarettes. Chuck notices a surprised expression on his buddies' faces. He asks: "What's a matter?" "Look behind you!" comes the reply. Five Germans are standing over them with fixed bayonets. Chuck recounts: "They took our helmets off, they took whatever we had and they said: "Raus!" and we start walking away from our line. I guess the officers were watching way up the hill. They called artillery over us. Not much over us! We could hear 'WEEEJJJJJJJJJ'. The Germans looked at each other, and we looked at each other. So we thought instead of standing around, we'd just turn around and start running for our positions. The Germans wanted to hide. By the time they looked at us, we were running. I never had my feet going so fast. And I ran like a mile and as I was going over the mount I heard the Germans' bullets: 'PING! PING!' We all got away."

Holes

Second only to his rifle, the infantryman's most important tool is his shovel. The M-1943 entrenching shovel (A) features a swiveling head that can be fully extended, angled as a hoe, or folded back for storage. The M-1943 gradually replaces the M-1910 shovel (B), although many soldiers prefer the T-handle of the older model.

Wherever a unit stops, the first order of business is usually digging in for concealment and protection against shelling and small arms. If they are only stopping for a few hours or to bivouac for the night, soldiers dig individual slit trenches about two foot wide, two foot deep and as long as the soldier is tall. Remembers William Campbell of the 28th Infantry Division: "It was like digging a grave."

If the position is to be held, one or two-men foxholes are dug about four to five feet deep, usually with a step at the bottom, upon which soldiers can sit down, or stand to stay out of pooling water or to fire their rifles. According to army manuals,[27] a foxhole with two feet of clearance above a crouching soldier protects him from tanks passing overhead, but German tankers learn to skid their treads over foxholes to collapse them and bury occupants alive.

The longer they remain in a defensive location the more elaborate their

underground "homes" become. Foxholes are improved with roofs made of logs, doors or corrugated steel taken from nearby buildings and covered with earth for protection against tree bursts and mortar shells. The floor is lined with hay or pine boughs. Soldiers carve out shelves for supplies, candles and ammunition. Frank Mareska of the 75th Infantry Division recalls that the much-dreaded German 88 guns left no time to duck: "You only venture out of your foxhole if it was necessary. Pissing or shitting had to be done either in a K or C-ration box, period! Renderings could then be thrown out over the parapet of your foxhole.[28]" Larger holes are dug for machine guns and mortar positions, sometimes, entire vehicles are entrenched. When visibility is limited by falling snow, fog or obscurity, companies dig listening slit trenches some distance outside their perimeter to post sentries.

Hard-frozen ground is doubly murderous for the infantry: It makes shells more deadly as they explode on the surface, rather than penetrate the ground, and it also makes it much more difficult to dig in. John McAuliffe of the 87th Infantry Division recalls that setting up a mortar position involves digging a large, two to three-foot deep circular entrenchment in addition to individual foxholes for the crew: "Sometimes we were digging a hole and we were almost done and they'd say: 'OK, we're moving out!'".

After a long day of fighting, many are too exhausted to dig. In some places, the frozen ground is simply too hard for the entrenching shovel and few men carry the cumbersome M1910 pick mattock (C). Most vehicles carry full-size shovels, axes and pickaxes. John Di Battista of the 4th Armored Division recalls: "The mattocks were heavy enough to go through the crust of ground. Once the crust was broken out, entrenching tools could do the job.[…] We were desperate hugging the ground waiting for our turn at a pick.[29]" Some units are provided with half-pound blocks of TNT with pull-type fuse lighters, fuses and blasting caps (D) to blast through the rock-hard crust of the frozen ground. An obvious disadvantage of the TNT method is the attention it draws. Rocco Moretto of the 1st Infantry Division recalls: "Everything was going beautifully but the TNT threw up heavy black smoke in the explosion areas. The enemy observing this quickly began to rake our positions with heavy concentrations of fire and we began to sustain heavy casualties.[30]"

Naturally, soldiers do not bother to fill their foxholes as they leave, consequently, Europe is riddled with millions of holes. It is not unusual for a foxhole to be occupied alternatively by American and German soldiers. After the war, It falls to landowners and farmers to fill in hundreds of thousands of foxholes and shell craters which are troublesome for machinery and hazardous to livestock. A post-war survey of the grounds of the Castle of Rolley, an area of about 730 acres near Bastogne, counts no less than 2,490 foxholes to fill in.[31]

Stanley Fink of the 2nd Infantry Division digs his hole near Wirtzfeld on January 30, 1945. U.S. National Archives.

Fly-Boys

The World War II generation grew up steeped in romantic accounts of legendary aviation pioneers such as Charles Lindbergh, Jimmy Doolittle and Amelia Earhart. Many draftees aspire to become fliers, but few are selected for the Aviation Cadet Training Program that forms pilots, navigators and bombardiers.

The debonair "knights of the sky", well groomed in tailored uniforms and leather jackets enjoy a privileged status among soldiers. They earn extra flight pay and are adulated by the public. In their magnificent aircraft, high above the earth, they are far-removed from the carnage and destruction they inflict. Wartime reporter Ernie Pyle wrote: "You approach death rather decently in the Air Forces. You die well-fed and clean-shaven, if that's any comfort. You're at the front only a few hours of the day, instead of day and night for months on end. In the evening you come back to something approximating a home and fireside.[32]" In return for these privileges, airmen routinely expose themselves to extremely perilous duty. One out of four airmen who fight in Europe is killed, and one out of five is taken prisoner.[3] Flying complex, high-performance aircraft is dangerous in itself. 14,903 airmen die on training missions in the United States. Close to half of the 40,000 airmen deaths are due to non-combat causes such as mechanical failures or navigation error.[33]

Aircrews crossing the channel from Great Britain wear inflatable "Mae Wests" life vests, so nicknamed because inflated, they evoke the famous actress' voluptuous figure. At high altitude, in unpressurized aircrafts,

temperatures dip as low as -50°F and low oxygen levels can kill in a matter of minutes. To survive these conditions, the airman's equipment includes a fleece-lined jacket (D) and a headset with an oxygen mask (E). The M3 bomber FLAK helmet (F) is similar to the M1 infantry helmet, but with hinged ear flaps to accommodate headsets.

As Hitler is hoping, limited visibility forces the Air Force to sit out the start of the Battle of the Bulge. Paul Priday of the 9th U.S. Air Force, stationed about 100 miles west of Bastogne, remembers the frustration of the aircrews: "Missions were scheduled and briefed each morning. Impatient air crews remained near their assigned aircraft, receiving repeated one hour delays until late afternoon when the mission would be officially scrubbed.[34]" When the sky finally clears on December 23, the USAF and RAF come out in force. Over the following five days, the USAF alone flies more than 16,000 sorties.[35] Richard Manchester of the 87th Infantry Division wrote: "After unremitting fog, one day it dawned clear without a cloud. The U.S. Army Air Force put thousands of planes up. B-17s were followed by B-26s and by P-38s. The sky was filled with contrails. Dug in on a hillside, we stood up in our foxholes and cheered.[36]"

On January 1, in an attempt to blunt the effect of the Allied Air Forces, the Luftwaffe simultaneously attacks U.S. air bases in the Netherlands, Belgium and France. The Germans destroy 127 Allied aircrafts parked on the ground, but within 24 hours, replacements are flown in from Great Britain. The Luftwaffe on the other hand, will never recover form the loss of 232 pilots and 300 airplanes, 100 of which are shot down by German flak gunners who have not been informed of the operation.[9]

Friendly fire between the US Air Force and US ground troops is frequent as well, so much so that infantrymen cynically dub the 9th U.S. Air Force the "American Luftwaffe". Navigation relies in large part on dead reckoning and the identification of land features. Patchy fog, low clouds and snow cover lead to errors, sometimes with catastrophic consequences. The double bombing of Malmedy is among the most tragic examples (See Page 73). On ground-support and interdiction missions, distinguishing friend from foe is tricky, particularly when both sides do their best to blend in with the snow. Jack Graber of the 75th Infantry Division recalls being attacked by American planes in Somme-Leuze on December 15: "These P-38s bombed and strafed our platoon, 3rd platoon. We dove in the ravine alongside the road, while the P-38 strafed the road hitting about 10 feet away. After about two or three passes, our platoon laid out the colors of the day. These (smoke grenade) colors were changed often and were meant for cases like this, to notify our planes that this is a friendly area. The P-38 immediately dispersed.[37]"

(A)

The crew of an M16 multiple motor gun carriage (See page 108) observes condensation trails that denote the intensity of aerial combats over the Ardennes on December 25, 1944. U.S. National Archives.

A Second Enemy

The Ardennes are often erroneously referred to as mountains in history books. If the region, famous for its wild boars, forests and deep valleys has something of an alpine character, it is probably the exceptionally harsh winter conditions that reinforced the impression of a mountainous region. For the unfortunate GIs fighting the Battle of the Bulge, the weather proves every bit as malevolent and deadly a foe as the Germans.

The start of the battle coincides with a period of intermittent rain, drizzle and fog. Spotty remnants of earlier snowfalls are present only at high elevations. Just as Hitler had hoped, this weather paralyzes Allied planes and hampers American artillery observers, but it takes a toll on the Germans as well. Until the ground would freeze later on, traveling cross-country is nearly impossible because the soil is saturated with rain. Military convoys churn country roads into quagmires. Even paved roads, which are fewer in those days, fare poorly under heavy armored vehicles, some weighting up to seventy tons. The cold drizzle makes life miserable for infantrymen on both sides. Uniforms and boots are soaked and caked with mud. Men become disoriented or separated in heavy fog. Incidences of friendly fire are frequent; soldiers stumble into enemy positions and the ensuing fighting at close range is confused and savage. Foxholes filled with water and mud cause trench foot (See page 112).

During the night of December 21 to December 22, almost a week into the battle, the arrival of an arctic front turns the rain to heavy snow. In the afternoon of the 23rd the sky clears and the temperature plummets. In the weeks that follow, more storms bring the snow total to several feet in some areas. The weather station of the town of Spa is one of very few that continues to gather weather data during the battle. In January, it records up to 20" of snow and temperatures as low as 0°F.[39]

GIs are poorly equipped and trained for winter conditions. General Omar Bradley would later write: "When the rain first came in November with a blast of wintry cold, our troops were ill-prepared for wintertime campaigning. This was traceable in part to the September crisis in supply for during our race to the Rhine, I had deliberately by-passed shipments of winter clothing in favor of ammunition and gasoline.[114]" To make things worse, many troops are rushed to the Ardennes before they can be issued what little cold-weather clothing is available. They find themselves trudging through slush and heavy snow and shivering in frigid foxholes for days on end in little more than summer uniforms. Overcoats, gloves, long underwear and galoshes eventually trickle through but, remembers Francis Gaudere of the 119th Infantry Division: "Before all that stuff came up, the rear echelon were all equipped with the clothes that we should have had." Infantrymen evacuated to hospitals are often upset to find out that nurses in the rear are better equipped for the cold than they are. Herb Adams of the 82nd Airborne Division recalls: "We didn't have any winter gear. [...] There was no long johns or anything else, so I put on my dress uniform and put the jumpsuit over it. We didn't even have overcoats." Dr. John Mc Auliffe of the 87th Infantry Division layered every article of clothing he owned: "I had two OD (Olive drab) pants, two OD shirts, a warm sweater, a Mackinaw jacket, an overcoat and then a wool scarf. I could hardly move!"

The cold becomes a near constant and painful hassle. John Cipolla of the 101st Airborne Division wrote: "The simplest task was difficult. Opening a can of K rations, re-tying a bootlace, or feeding rounds into a clip with numb hands could be infuriating difficult.[40]" Frederick Smallwood of the 106th Infantry Division wrote: "Our pants did not have zippers but had a button fly. My fingers were stiff from cold but I finally got them unbuttoned and, after I finished, I couldn't button them back.[41]"

During the long nights, the cold turns deadly. Raymond Wenning of the 30th Infantry Division recounts: "It was so cold I would hock down in the foxhole on my heels, and shiver so hard that my teeth would rattle and my knees would get sore and hurt just from shaking. There were at least three nights I thought I would just freeze to death and not wake up.[42]" Ray Huckaby of the 35th Infantry Division explains: "Your muscles will quiver steadily so that even if you doze, your body will continue to shiver on and on. You become afraid after a while to let yourself go sound asleep for fear that your heart and metabolism will slow just a little bit more and you will never awaken.[43]" In November and December of 1944, casualties attributed to the cold amount to 23,000 men, almost all of them combat infantrymen.[44] Remembers Chester Wenc of the 106th Infantry Division: "They died sitting in their foxhole, they froze stiff. Once they fell asleep, they'd die." William Campbell of the 28th Infantry marvels at what the human body can get used to. He remembers a surreal instance when, struck by the beauty of the snow-covered landscape, he became oblivious to the cold for a moment and stopped shivering: "Here I am, sitting in the snow. There was a lot of snow. And you know what it's like when there is a bright moon and it casts shadows through the trees and you could see the snow sparkle. It was like a Christmas postcard. I'm not even cold. I think I had frozen feet, but it showed up later."

Some 15,000 men have to be evacuated due to trench foot or frozen feet. Frigid temperatures sharply reduce the odds of survival for the wounded. Immobilized, lying on the frozen ground and weakened by the loss of blood they quickly go into shock. The delicate life-saving work of the medics is made more difficult by the numbing cold. Many have to keep morphine syrettes tucked in their underwear and bottles of plasma under their armpits to prevent them from freezing.

The weather is hard on the equipment as well. Vehicles refuse to start because the cold weakens batteries and thickens engine oil. Some drivers resort to lighting gasoline fires under their engine or leaving their vehicle running 24 hours a day for fear that it could not be started quickly in an emergency. The wheels of vehicles and artillery pieces sink into mud or slush, which then freezes solid overnight. Inside tanks, frozen condensation from the men's breath seizes up turret traverse and gun mechanisms. Snow, mud or rain seep into ammunition clips and belts, then freeze and jam weapons. Many men find out the hard way that if they have the opportunity to step into a warm place, they must leave their weapons outside, otherwise condensation can freeze on the frigid steel and seize the weapon's bolt. In intense cold, gun oil becomes as sticky as heavy grease. Charles Miller of the 75th Infantry Division recalls that the M1 rifle's bolt could be force-closed manually, until after a few rounds were fired, it became warm enough to function normally, but automatic firearms that fire from an open bolt such as the BAR or submachine gun become inoperable. He wrote: "I advised the men carrying them to remove the cartridge clips from the weapons, stuff toilet paper into the receiver and set it on fire. I did likewise with my submachine gun and thus we succeeded in warming them enough so that they started working.[45]"

Pfc. William Mercer, driver with the 90th Infantry Division, thaws brake parts on his vehicle with a blowtorch. U.S. Army photo

Ida's Monkey

Five-year-old Ida and her brother José live with their grandmother in the small town of Joubiéval. Fearful of the bombardments, the three spend much of their days in the relative safety of the basement. One evening, as they venture up the basement stairs, they come face to face with American soldiers (likely from the 83rd Infantry Division) who were settling in the house for the night. Ida is shy and somewhat afraid of the soldiers, but she is also curious. She is particularly intrigued by a black soldier. Until then, she only had seen representation of black people in books about the Congo, a Belgian colony at the time. To ease the little girl's fears, the black soldier pulls out a little monkey puppet from his bag and starts playing with her. One can imagine that it did not take him long to put a smile on the little girl's face. It is also likely that Ida and her brother enjoyed their first taste of chocolate and candy in a long time that evening. Ida never forgot this extraordinary encounter with the kind-hearted American soldiers. She treasured the little monkey puppet for the rest of her life.

Ida's monkey is exhibited at the Bulge Relics Museum in Joubiéval.

Gloves and Mittens

Standard-issue gloves (A) are made of woolen cloth reinforced with leather palms. John McAuliffe of the 87th Infantry Division recalls: "The gloves were terrible because you were always doing something. You know, packing and loading the jeep. You wore holes right through the gloves. Your fingers would be cold!" The mittens (B), designed for mountain troops, are effective against the cold, but only available in small quantities. They are a combination of knit wool inserts and water-resistant shells made of cotton poplin and leather. The trigger-finger allows soldiers to fire their rifles without exposing their hands to the cold, but both mittens and gloves have to come off for such tasks as reloading or throwing grenades, etc. Many soldiers wear hand-knitted gloves (C) send from home or donated by locals..

Pfc. Arlow Jensen of the 83rd Infantry Division enjoys a sleigh ride near Houffalize, Belgium on December 10, 1944. U.S. National Archives.

Winter Hats

The headgear shown here is among the most common in the winter of 1944. The wool hood (D) is originally intended to be worn in combination with the gas mask as protection against vesicant gases but it proves much more useful against the cold. The pile field cap (E) features an artificial fur lining and generous ear flaps that make it a favorite of vehicle drivers. The wind-proof cotton poplin hood (F) and wool knit "beanie" (G) are designed to be worn under the M1 helmet. The beanie includes a rigid brim and a border that can be turned down over the ears. The Field Cap (H) is designed as an all-season hat that can be worn with or without the helmet. It features a fold-down, flannel-lined curtain to cover the ears.

Elvire Herbillon Remembers

Elvire grew up in the town of Awirs, Belgium, where her parents ran a small grocery store. When the Germans invade Belgium in 1940, she is a seventeen-year-old nursing student at the *Hopital des Anglais* in Liège. As the city comes under attack, she participates in the evacuation of another larger hospital. Patients are transported across the city on gurneys, the wheels of which get caught in the tramway rails. Some of her fellow nurses, startled by gunfire, seek refuge on doorsteps. Elvire recounts: "When we arrived at a bridge, we were told: 'Hurry up, the bridge is going to blow up!' So we did what we could and we made it across just in time." Among the flood of war casualties, Elvire remembers a man whose leg she was asked to hold while it was amputated. She explains: "Sometimes, it seems like I can still feel the weight of that

Elvire keeps a few mementos from the war, including a little piece of wartime soap formulated with rock dust. She explains that the rock-hard soap hardly lathered at all, but would last for months. She also kept a booklet of coupons for free supplies that, as a humanitarian aid, she distributed to pregnant women.

leg." She also remembers a young boy with a black velvet suit and his mother who refused to let the nurses take his young, bullet-riddled body to the morgue. Extra mattresses are installed directly on the floor to accommodate the overflow of patients. Electricity and gas outages are frequent and the hospital is critically short on supplies and drugs.

Fortunately, Elvire also remembers lighter moments. On one occasion, the nurses help a sick prisoner escape by giving the German guard posted at his door a heavy dose of what they call "the eleven o'clock bouillon", a sedative they ordinarily give to patients in the evening to help them sleep. Elvire recalls that as she and her friends walk past military barracks occupied by the Germans, they sing an old song in Walloon (a local dialect): "Eat more pie, eat more pie, to make sure that you all die!" Germans soldier, who do not understand a word, are applauding the young singers.

Elvire has two brothers: Albert, a soldier, spends the entire war in Germany as a prisoner of war. Jean, the youngest, is suspected of having assassinated a Nazi-sympathizing mayor by the name of Grimont. Hunted by the Germans, he flees to France on his bicycle. The family would not hear from him for the next six months.

Near the end of the war, Elvire works as a humanitarian aid, which allows her to return home every evening and take care of her ailing parents. During the Battle of the Bulge, she travels the countryside on her bicycle to distribute food and medical supplies. She has to stop periodically to scrape the snow that accumulates under the mudguard and blocks the wheels. As the Americans regain ground, she pedals deeper and deeper into the Ardennes to help distribute clothing and blankets provided by the Americans.

Paul Mardaga, a young Belgian medical student who would become her husband, enlists in the American Army as a translator for the Medical Corps. Among the few mementos that he kept from the war is a dog tag (A) that he received from a mortally wounded soldier during the Battle of the Bulge. Elvire explains that he told her husband, who was doing his best to comfort him: "I don't have relatives. Here, take it. You are my brother." Her husband also kept a small piece of an observation airplane (B) that he received as a good luck charm from a downed pilot he rescued.

Thompson Submachine Gun

With the advent of trench warfare during World War I, retired General John T. Thompson sees a large potential market for a new type of close-quarter, rapid-fire gun he calls "trench sweeper". However, the development of his submachine gun would not be completed before the end of the war. During the 1930s, the Thompson submachine gun earns the nickname the "Chicago Typewriter" in the hands of prohibition era criminal gangs and depression bank robbers. The Thompson, more commonly referred to as the "Tommy" during the war, fires .45 pistol rounds, the same rounds as the M1911 colt pistol (See page 83). The M1928A1 version shown here is an early war model that can be loaded with fifty-round drums or straight magazines with maximum capacities of twenty or thirty rounds. The later M1 variant features a simplified sight and firing mechanism, the elimination of the cooling fins on the barrel and the relocation of the cocking handle to the left side of the gun. The Tommy gun is a blowback automatic firearm. This means that the reloading mechanism is powered by the force of the shell casing pushing back on the breech when the gun is fired. In fully automatic mode, the Tommy fires 600 to 700 rounds per minute. This high rate of fire and the sharp angle of the stock give the gun a tendency to climb and fire high. The Tommy gun is expensive and heavy for its size. It is issued primarily to officers who do not need the power of the Garand rifle, or to soldiers that are expected to fight at close range in confined spaces.

The 24th Cavalry Reconnaissance Squadron links up with the 507th Parachute Infantry Regiment in La Roche on January 14, 1945.
U.S. Army photo.

Cartridge Belt and Bandoleer

The designation of the .30-06 cartridge (A) is indicative of its 0.30" caliber and adoption by the US Army in 1906. The M1 Garand rifle, the BAR and the .30 Browning machine gun all fire the same .30-06 cartridge. This makes supplying infantrymen squads simpler and makes it possible for soldiers to redistribute ammunition as necessary. The cartridge belt shown here holds ten M1 rifle 8-round clips (B). Riflemen ammunition is delivered in crates of disposable cotton bandoleers (C), each containing six clips (D). A rifleman with a full ammunition belt and two extra bandoleers over his shoulders carries 176 cartridges that weight approximately twelve pounds. The lubricating oil container and cleaning patches (E) are sized to fit in one of the cartridge belt pockets.

Gas Mask

The lightweight service gas mask, M3 (A) and M6 carrier (B) or other variants are standard-issue equipment. The face piece is connected by a rubber hose to a filter canister that remains in the bag while the mask is in use. Soldiers are also issued anti-dim cloths (C) to prevent the eyepieces from fogging up, a waterproofing kit (D) and individual protective covers (E). These are large, cape-like plastic bags with see-through tops. Soldiers can kneel or sit on the ground and cover themselves completely for protection against aerosolized agents.

Gas mask drills are a staple of basic training. The gas chamber trial is a right of passage during which the instructor highlights the importance of proper procedures by momentarily exposing the trainees to the painful effects of the tear-gas.

By late 1944, with no recorded instance of German chemical attacks in combat, GIs come to view their gas masks as a useless burden. Many discard them, but keep the handy carrier and use the protective covers as rain capes, foxhole or ground covers. On December 17, 1944, Allan Stein is rushed to the Ardennes with the 82nd Airborne Division. He wrote: "I had just received a package from home with four cartons of cigarettes. Where the hell do you put four cartons with the other stuff we had? Naturally, I somehow lost my gas mask. The container was a very nice place for all those little oddities.[46]" Sgt Henry Mooseker of the 87th Infantry Division lists among his unit's typical possessions: "A gas mask carrier that had long had the gas mask removed and that now served well to carry cigarettes, K-rations, condoms, and the wax candles that we used to heat food with, toilet articles and any loot we could eat.[47]"

During the Battle of the Bulge, it is feared that an increasingly desperate Hitler might yet resort to chemical warfare. On January 7, a report to Washington by Eisenhower's headquarters states: "This offensive is an all-out effort in which Hitler will employ any weapon. It has always been appreciated that Germany might initiate gas warfare to obtain a decisive result. The battle having gone badly, Hitler may regard this as the moment. We should not overlook the chaos which would result among the civilian population in NW Europe with the possible employment of a gas warhead in V-1 and V-2.[44]" Fortunately, these fears were never realized.

Pvt. Adam Davis and T/S Milford Sillars of the 28th Infantry Division in Bastogne on December 19, 1944. U.S. Army photo.

U.S. Carbine, Caliber .30, M1

The Carbine is issued as a lightweight alternative to the Garand rifle to soldiers who carry heavy or bulky equipment such as radios, mortars, bazookas, machine guns, etc. The carbine is about half the weight of the Garand rifle and 8 inches shorter. It is also issued to officers and rear personnel such as drivers, cooks, company clerks, etc, who are not normally expected to confront the enemy, but who might need something more than a pistol for self defense. An even more compact version of the carbine with a folding stock is developed for paratroopers (See page 110).

The carbine with its small .30 round is considerably less powerful than the Garand rifle. Some soldiers deride it as a "peashooter",

or are reluctant to carry it because they fear they might be mistaken for officers by German snipers. In reality, in many situations, the carbine is just as effective as the Garand, and its lighter ammunition can be carried in much larger quantities.

The operating mechanism of the Carbine is similar to that of the Garand. Firing it is extremely simple: One simply has to insert a 15-round magazine, pull the operating slide back, and squeeze the trigger. The two-magazine pouch (A) is designed to be carried on a pistol belt, but GIs soon discover that it fits perfectly around the stock on the carbine (See photo).

One of the carbine's designers was known as "Carbine" Williams. Interestingly enough, Williams was a former moonshiner who had honed his skills as a gun maker in the machine shop of a prison where he was serving a jail sentence for murder.

Medium Tank, M4 "Sherman"

The Sherman tank is among the most iconic tanks of World War II. With about 50,000 built during the war, it is the most common Allied tank. Production of the Sherman begins in 1942. Many specifications are dictated by considerations that have little to do with its fighting role. The Sherman has to be economical and easy to mass-produce. Because it is to be deployed overseas, it has to be lightweight and easy to fit through the hatches of freight ships, hence its boxy proportions, relatively light armor, stubby gun and four heavy lifting rings welded onto the hull. Among the greatest qualities of the Sherman tank are its mechanical simplicity and reliability. Among its weaknesses are its relatively thin frontal armor and underpowered gun.

The Sherman's (arguably unjustified) reputation for bursting into flame earns it the nickname of "Ronson", a brand of cigarette lighters. One on one in the open, it stands little chance against the better armed and armored German Panther or Tiger tanks. Working in packs however, it can maneuver to hit German tanks from their vulnerable sides or rears. Later versions of the Sherman feature thicker armor and extra plating welded in front and to the sides to protect the driver and co-driver. Crews often supplement their armor with sandbags, spare tracks, or even concrete. A full Sherman tank crew consists in five men: A tank commander, a driver, assistant driver, gunner and gun loader.

Men of the 82nd Airborne Division and an M4 Sherman tank of the 740th Tank Battalion join forces near Herresbach, Belgium in January 1945. The tracks of the Sherman are fitted with "duckbills", extensions that widen the tracks to provide better traction on the snow. U.S. Army photo.

Above: Soldiers of the 5th Armored Division draw names for pass privilege near Eupen on November 20, 1944. Bottom: Pvt. James Curran of Chicago on a 3-day pass in an unnamed Belgian city on December 12, 1944. U.S. Army photos.

Rest and Relaxation

Handed out at the whim of commanding officers, passes and furloughs are never guaranteed. Because passes typically cover 72 hours or less, they only provide access to local towns. Furloughs are equivalent to vacations, they span up to several weeks, sometimes long enough for soldiers to return home. New recruits are usually granted furloughs after basic training, or right before they are sent overseas. Francis Gaudier, a radio operator for the 119th Infantry Division recalls that he did not receive a single pass during the eleven months he spent on the line.

A favorite, albeit illegal way to finance a furlough, is to sell cigarettes on the black market. A soldier can purchase a carton for 50¢ at an Army PX (See page 115), and at the first large train station, sell it on the black market for up to $20.[44] For an American soldier serving in Belgium, a pass is typically spent in cities like Brussels, Liège, Spa, Luxembourg, or Eupen. A furlough usually means a trip to Paris. Unlike most large cities in Europe, Paris is left mostly unscathed by the war. Among the must-see Paris attractions are the Eiffel Tower, the Arc de Triomphe, the bare-breasted dancers of the "Folies Bergères" and the nightlife of Pigalle, pronounced "pig alley" by the soldiers.

The typical infantry division consists of three regiments that are rotated in and out of combat. In theory, while two regiments are on combat duty, one is held back in reserve and allowed to rest in the rear. Prior to the Battle of the Bulge, picturesque towns such as Laroche-en-Ardennes, Spa and Clervaux, that attract tourists in peacetime, are ideal for rest and relaxation. Soldiers are offered such luxuries as hot showers, haircuts and real beds. In conjunction with the USO and the Red Cross, "Morale" officers organize leisure activities such as sports, movies, dances, religious services and education opportunities, depending on available amenities. Financed in large part by profit from PX stores, these activities are attempts to improve the morale of the soldiers and to keep them away from excessive alcohol and debauchery. Boxing fights are very much appreciated, not only as a form of entertainment, but also as benign way to settle long-simmering disputes between soldiers.

Herb Adams of the 82nd Parachute Infantry Division Remembers

Herbert Adams is born in 1924 in Waterville, Maine to a Canadian lumberjack who immigrated to the United States to find work. By the time he is five years old, he and his five siblings are orphaned. Herb is adopted by an uncle, a barn builder in Norridgewock, Maine. After he graduates from high school in 1942, he goes to work for the South Portland Shipyard. Herb is anxious to serve in the military, but his employment in a war-critical industry prevents him doing so. On Christmas of 1942, he presents himself at a draft board and deliberately omits to state his current job. Herb is sent to a Coastal Artillery Barrage Balloon Battalion. Finding his assignment boring and eager to play a more active role in the fight, he requests a transfer to the paratroopers.

Herb remembers a physically and mentally grueling training regimen at Fort Benning in Georgia with the 504th Parachute Infantry Regiment: "I had already gone through what was called basic training. It was no training at all compared to what I went through in the paratroopers." The recruits never walk but run everywhere and all the time, and sergeants dole out push-ups at the drop of a hat. The hand-to-hand combat and bayonet trainings are so intense that many are injured and some die. Herb recounts:"You'd get knocked out, they'd just drag your ass onto the grass somewhere and when you'd come to, they'd tell you to get back in there." Herb would later credit his survival in many perilous situations to the paratroopers' rigorous training and physical conditioning.

After his five qualifying parachute jumps, Herb receives a one-week furlough to visit his wife Beverly in Maine before he is shipped to North Africa, then to Italy where he takes part in the Battle of Anzio. In the spring of 1944, stationed in England, Herb volunteers for fifteen night-time parachute jumps to train aircraft navigators for the invasion of Normandy. Herb explains: "You weren't on the ground five minutes, but you knew where you were, because someone with a pitchfork or a shotgun wanted to know what the hell you were doing there. So once you convinced the Brit what it was all about, you'd look at the map. Some nights we'd be twenty miles from where we were supposed to be." Herb's first combat jump does not take place over France as he had expected, but over the Netherlands during *Operation Market Garden*.

At the onset of the Battle of the Bulge, Herb is stationed in Sissonne, France.

Around midnight on December 18, 1944 comes the order to prepare to leave in six hours. Because the 82nd Airborne Division is slated for deployment in the Pacific, it has not been equipped with winter clothing. Herb and his fellow paratroopers gather what ammunition and field rations they can. Some who have turned in their weapons for repair are unarmed. The men are loaded onto open-top truck trailers. They are packed so tightly, remembers Herb, that there is no room to sit. The half-frozen paratroopers are dropped off in Werbomont, around 11:00 the following evening. Herb recalls: "You haven't had a chance to sleep. You jumped off the goddamned trucks. Now we had to walk about eight miles and you immediately go into attack against the Germans." Herb's regiment confronts the spearhead of the 1st SS Panzer Division in Rahier and then again in Cheneux in what would turn out to be the 82nd Airborne Division's most brutal fighting of the war.

By Christmas, the weather changes from drizzle and fog to heavy snow and frigid temperatures. Herb nearly loses both feet to frostbites. Short of ammunition and food and wearing little more than their summer uniforms, the paratroopers relentlessly fight some of Hitler's toughest troops. Herb remembers a lull in particularly brutal assault: "It was time to have a break, a lunch break and I was over here and there were dead Germans. What the hell, they made good seats. I sat down on a German, and he was still warm, and I ate my lunch. It was one of a few things that I did that I'm not proud of. Shooting him was one thing, but using his body for a seat... When I think back, it wasn't the right thing to do."

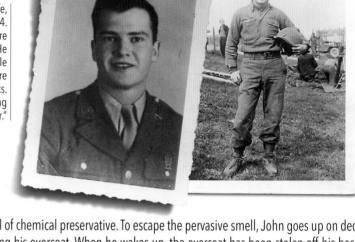

John McAuliffe was born on October 6, 1923 in Brooklyn, New York, the son of sculptor Florence McAuliffe. He and his three siblings lost their parents at an early age. John is a pre-medical student at Holy Cross College in Worcester, Massachusetts when Japanese planes bomb Pearl Harbor. As soon as he graduates in June of 1944, John is drafted into the Army. He trains for seventeen weeks as a mortar man and heavy machine gunner at Camp Wheeler, Georgia. During basic training, John is selected as a coach on the rifle range. He recalls: "They had guys firing at targets and I had to lay besides them and make sure they had the sling on and everything right, and aiming right and doing all that. All day! When I got back at night, I couldn't hear anything in the barracks." John keeps his hearing loss to himself for fear of being discharged from the Army. He is enjoying a furlough at home after the end of his training when he reads about the Battle of the Bulge in the newspaper. Upon his return to duty he is immediately shipped across the Atlantic from New York to Glasgow. The 18,000 men on the Queen Mary have received all new cloth-

Left: John McAuliffe, freshly drafted in 1944. Right: John somewhere in Germany in 1945. He points out: "If I look a little chubby, it's because I wore two trousers and two shirts. We all lost weight during the war."

ing with a strong smell of chemical preservative. To escape the pervasive smell, John goes up on deck and takes a nap wearing his overcoat. When he wakes up, the overcoat has been stolen off his back. During the rest of the trip his helmet and blankets are stolen as well. John remembers: "We got on these boxcars on a freight train. No heat, no food, standing, no light. It took us three days and nights to get to Metz, and I froze all the way over." John is attached to a mortar team of the 87th Infantry Division: "Being a replacement, I was the low man on the totem pole. My job was ammunition bearer. Each round weights 6.7 pounds. I carried six of them, that's forty-two pounds. Besides all my gear, heavy overcoat, galoshes and a carbine."

Since the mortars with a range of up to 3,300 yards are usually set some distance back from the front line, the mortar teams have it a little better than other infantrymen. On occasion John and his squad find refuge in barns or farmhouses. He remembers: "We'd take over barns mostly, because people didn't like us going into their houses. Most of the houses in Belgium had a little barn attached to them where they had cows in the winter. It wasn't an awful dirty smell, but there was an animal smell that pervaded the whole house." John remembers that civilians were usually happy to see the American soldiers. He recalls: "They were surprised to see how young we were."

Among John's most vivid memories of the Ardennes is an action on the Siegfried line near the town of Ormont, Germany. He is sent running a distance of about a quarter mile across an open field when German shells start falling all around him. He remembers thinking that if a piece of shrapnel were to hit one of the mortar shells he was carrying, he would instantly disappear. When he finally makes it to the edge of the woods, German tree bursts start coming in. He takes cover under a large fallen tree: "The guy sitting next to me, when we came out, he was holding his knee which was blown up. He was holding his knee and screaming and yelling." John and his unit stumble upon an abandoned German bunker where they spend the night safe and secure. The next morning, the sergeant sends John on a detail, but he is so cold that it takes him a half hour to buckle his overshoes. John recalls: "My hands were so numb, I was like a kid in Kindergarten trying to tie his shoes."

After the war, John finally seeks help for the hearing loss he suffered at the rifle range and while firing thousands of mortar shells without hearing protection. Though he never recovered, he enjoyed a long and successful career as a dentist. John adds modestly: "But a lot of veterans had it harder than me, they had no arms or legs." Among his patients were the children of his famous namesake Brigadier General Anthony McAuliffe.

A Belgian girl is happy to give directions to an American jeep on January 1945. American soldiers often welded vertical wire cutters to the front bumper of their jeeps, because they feared that Germans might stretch wires across roads to decapitate them. U.S. National Archives.

Truck, ¼ ton, 4x4 "Jeep"

In 1940, the U.S. Army calls for bids on a light, four-wheel-drive utility and reconnaissance vehicle. Within fifty days, the American Bantam Car Company submits a prototype, which would eventually evolve into the iconic Jeep. But the company does not have the production capacity to meet the enormous demand, so the War Department contracts the Willys Overland Motors and the Ford Motor Company to produce the jeep and encourage them to incorporate their own improvements. More than 650,000 Jeeps are built during the war. Clever design features allow the jeep to be stacked for transport, or shipped in compact crates. The Jeep serves in all corners of the world and is adapted for a variety of roles including reconnaissance, litter carrier, communications wire laying, artillery towing, snow plowing,etc.

War correspondent Ernie Pyle wrote about the Jeep: "It does everything. It goes everywhere. It's as faithful as a dog, strong as a mule, and as agile as a goat. It constantly carries twice what it was designed for and keeps going." But he also complained: "I wish they could somehow have fixed the jeep so that at certain speeds the singing of those heavy tires hadn't sounded exactly like an approaching airplane.[48]"

The Execution of Private Eddie Slovik

In the chaos of combat and rapid troop movements, thousands of soldiers are lost, left behind, attached to other units, or otherwise become separated from their unit. Consequently, men who go AWOL (Absent Without Leave) are given considerable leeway. If they rejoin their units within a month, and sometimes much longer, they are not usually listed as deserters, so long as they come up with a somewhat plausible excuse. Many soldiers find themselves separated from their units without intention of deserting, but after enjoying the generosity of local hosts, they are reluctant to go back to the line. Soon after their liberations, a number of European cities experience surges in crime due to gangs of battle-hardened American deserters who, among other nefarious activities, sell stolen U.S. Army supplies on the black market. Plagued by American gang activity, Paris become known for a time as "Chicago-sûr-Seine.[44]" Of the nearly 50,000 Americans deserters, 21,000 are court-martialed and convicted, 49 are sentenced to death and only one is executed.[3]

Eddie Slovik is born in 1920 in Detroit Michigan to a working-class family. From the age of twelve, his life is marred by petty crimes and arrests. When Japan declares war on the United States, Slovik is classified as unfit for military service because he is serving a prison sentence. Upon his parole in 1942, he finds work and marries and by late 1943, he is reclassified and drafted into the Army. He arrives in France as a replacement in August 1944 and is affected to the 28th Infantry Division. On his way to his unit, he and a friend become separated from their group during an artillery barrage. The two go AWOL for six weeks before finally rejoining their outfit. Slovik immediately requests to be reassigned to non-combat duty stating that he is too scared to fight. When his request is denied, he simply walks away from his unit and turns himself in at the first opportunity. Slovak feels certain that his desertion will result in a prison sentence and a dishonorable discharge, prospects that don't daunt him at all, given his judicial history. He voluntarily composes and signs a confession that states among other things: "I'll run away again if I have to go out there.[49]"

Slovik is given several opportunities to avoid court-martial on the condition that he rejoins a fighting unit but he persists, confident that he is beating the system. Unfortunately, he has gravely miscalculated. His criminal record, the fact that he has never experienced combat, and the unapologetic confession he composed and signed are so many aggravating factors. Perhaps worst of all, his court-martial takes place in November,1944, at a time when American forces suffer catastrophic losses in the Hurtgen Forest and cases of desertion and battle fatigue are reaching alarming levels. Slovik is sentenced to death. General Norman Cota, Slovik's Division Commander approves the verdict. He would later state: "If I had let Slovik accomplish his purpose, I don't know how I could have gone up to the line and looked a good soldier in the face.[50]" Slovik fully expects his sentence to be commuted, as were those of all other deserters up to that point, but the verdict reaches the desk of General Eisenhower at the height of the Battle of the Bulge, when troop morale is at an all-time low. On December 24, Eisenhower approves the death sentence, noting that it is necessary to set an example for other would-be deserters.[51]

Eddie Slovik is executed by firing squad on January 31, 1945 in Sainte-Marie-aux-Mines, France. Shortly before his execution, he protests: "They just need to make an example out of somebody and I'm it because I'm an ex-con. I used to steal things when I was a kid, and that's what they are shooting me for.[49]"

Knit for Victory

The War Department encourages American women to do their part for the war effort by sending hand-knitted garments to sons, grandsons, brothers or husbands serving overseas. First Lady Eleanor Roosevelt champions the cause by appearing in public and in the press knitting for the Armed Forces. The American Red Cross organizes war relief knitting clubs all across America. Newspapers, magazines and a multitude of publications offer instructions and patterns for knitting army-sanctioned sweaters, wristlets, socks, balaclavas, scarves, etc. The promotional pamphlet on the right, titled *How to Knit for Victory* is published by a soap maker. Wool manufacturers capitalize by marketing yarn dyed to Army specifications and labeled with patriotic themes.

Mrs. Myrtle Ormsbee of East Montpelier, Vermont knits pullovers for the Red Cross in 1942. U.S. Library of Congress photo.

The *Red Ball Express*

The Allies' victory in World War II owes much to America's enormous capacity for industrial production. American factories, entirely safe from bombings and bustling with a highly motivated and healthy labor force produce prodigious quantities of vehicles, fuel, weapons, bombs and ammunition. This enormous flow of supplies from what becomes known as the American "home front" results in overwhelming firepower on the front lines. According to General Omar Bradley's autobiography, in the fall of 1944 the twenty-eight divisions in France and Belgium consume a staggering 20,000 tons of supplies every single day.[2]

To transport these supplies to the front, the army cannot rely on the railroads or harbor installations that have been destroyed either by Allied bombs or by retreating German forces. Most of the supplies must be brought in all the way from the beaches of Normandy by trucking companies. As the front lines move ever deeper into Europe, supply lines are stretched to their limits and shortages soon threaten to bring the Allied progress to a halt.

On August 25, 1944, the Transportation Corps launches the *Red Ball Express*, an elaborate trucking operation devised to alleviate supply problems. All available military trucks and drivers are pressed into the operation. Athanace "Joe" Landry, a truck driver for the 776th Anti Aircraft Artillery Battalion remembers: "We'd set our guns for a week or two and Patton didn't want any of these trucks idle. So he got all us guys that were truck drivers sitting around doing nothing for a week or two, to go on the *Red Ball Express*." Trucks are loaded at massive supply depots, the largest of which is located in Saint-Lô, France. In addition to their cargo, trucks carry enough jerrycans of fuel to get to their destination and come back. Traffic is routed to a dedicated network of one-way roads where no other type of traffic is allowed. MPs direct traffic at key junctions and post thousands of directional signs. Joe remembers very difficult conditions in the early days of the *Red Ball Express*: "You very seldom had a good meal. We were eating K-rations and that stuff. And you would go for a week or two without taking a bath or shaving. We used to drive twelve, fifteen hours with two drivers and we never stopped. One guy would get real close to the steering wheel, and the other would sit behind him and we'd just switch without out stopping."

The main truck of the U.S. Army is the 2 1/2 ton GMC better known as the "Deuce-and-a-half". It is a six-speed, six-wheel-drive truck with a top speed of about 44 mph.

As all soldiers do, drivers find clever ways to improve their lot. They find that the canvas over their trucks forms a sort of hammock where they take turns sleeping even as the truck is speeding along. Joe Landry warms up cans of beans and franks over the engine manifold and heats water in a helmet hung in the path of the exhaust. He also discovers that he can tune in music on his field radio. Arrived at their destination, trucks are unloaded quickly. Joe fondly remembers a particularly effective way of unloading 500lb bombs, and the panicked reaction of the soldiers witnessing the procedure for the first time: "We'd back up to a field, drop the tailgate, back up, hit the brake, and they'd all come rolling right off." At times, trucks are expected to deliver supplies directly to men on the front lines. Joe remembers chasing General Patton's Third Army tanks with a load of gasoline: "He was moving so fast, that you'd get to where you were supposed to drop it off, and there'd be an officer waiting there telling us they'd gone up ahead. We'd drive down the road and find a tank out of gas. We'd gas it up and leave and we'd go find another one." On return trips, trucks transport empty jerrycans, shell casings, German prisoners or the bodies of dead soldiers. Joe remembers a load of American nurses heading back to a rest camp: "They all had coveralls, the one-piece uniforms that the nurses had. We stopped at a convent somewhere in Belgium for the nurses to rest a little bit. At first the nuns wouldn't let them in because they thought they were camp followers."

Record keeping is lax or nonexistent and because commodities like gasoline, soap, coffee and cigarettes command exorbitant prices on the black market, corruption and theft are widespread. Joe remembers a particular sergeant who oversaw German prisoners of war loading the trucks in Saint-Lô: "If you got a bottle of cognac for the Sergeant, you'd get an extra case of this or an extra case of that." There are instances of civilians, usually women or small children stepping in front of truck in an effort to stop them and beg for food.[52] In extreme cases, entire trucks and their cargo disappear. Joe recalls: "The drivers would come back and say: 'my truck broke down here or there and I went back and it was gone.'" Eventually, as a way to limit this kind of abuse, trucks are organized into convoys with officers or MPs in jeeps at both ends.

Given the crucial importance of logistical support, trucks

Above: Corporal Charles H. Johnson of the 783rd Military Police directs convoys bound for Alençon, France on September 5, 1944. Top right: Two *Red Ball Express* drivers are repairing a 2.5-ton truck while a third keeps watch for enemy planes with his .50 Browning heavy machine gun. U.S. National Archives Photos.
Right: The letters on the Red Ball Express patch stand for Transportation Corps Motor Transportation Service.

play as vital a role as the infantry, tanks and airplanes they support. The drivers are overworked and sleep-deprived. The convoys often transport dangerous loads of gasoline, ammunition and bombs. They are strafed by German airplanes and sometimes mistaken for German convoys by their own fighter-bombers. Some convoys come close enough to the front lines to be shelled by German artillery.

The *Red Ball Express* takes a serious toll on the vehicles as well. Repair depots located strategically along the way are backlogged with thousands of trucks awaiting repairs. French roads are generally unpaved, and the overloaded trucks run almost around the clock. Gearboxes are abused by volunteer drivers with little experience. Flat tires are such a crippling problem that the Army designs special trucks with magnetic sweepers to pick up shrapnel, barbed wire, and empty ration cans that litter the roads. In its first month, the operation wears out 40,000 tires.[52]

By the end of the *Red Ball Express* on November 16, 1944, about 410,000 tons have been transported.[53] The actual *Red Ball Express* ends a full month before the Battle of the Bulge, but the name becomes synonymous with similar operations that go on until the end of the war, including the Lion Express between Bayeux and Brussels and the ABC Express between Antwerp, Brussels and Charleroi.[53]

Joe Landry is one of six siblings in the service during the war. Soon after being drafted to Fort Devens, Massachusetts, Joe's outfit is transferred to Camp Davis, North Carolina to form the new 776th Anti-Aircraft Artillery Battalion. On the third day at Camp Davis, in spite of warnings never to volunteer for anything, Joe steps forward as a truck driver. Thus, he bypasses much of the drudgery of basic training. Joe remembers:"They were just forming this outfit and they had to go and pick up the supplies and get everything. While the other guys were running in the woods I was driving around."

In March of 1944, the 776th is shipped to England and tasked with protecting Plymouth harbor from German air raids. At the end of July, Joe drives his truck off the ramps of an LST (Landing Ship Troops) in about four feet of water on Omaha Beach in Normandy, France. He remembers observing the tragic bombing of St-Lo where many American soldiers, including General McNair were killed by their own bombs: "I saw the bombs falling and once in a while an airplane would come down. We were in Isigny. We're probably ten miles away. You could feel the ground shake."

Joe's job consists in transporting anti aircraft batteries and their crews from one location to the next. He explains: "We'd set our

Not all civilians are pleased with the arrival of their American liberators. The knife above, which Joe keeps as a souvenir, was thrown at him by a Frenchman as he was driving by. Fortunately, it harmlessly hit the window frame and was found on the running board. Left: By sheer luck, Joe came across his brother Harold near Verdun France in November 1944. Center: Joe drove the GMC CCKW 2½ ton 6×6 truck commonly known as the "deuce and a half". Right: 18-year-old Joe Landry in 1943.

guns for a week or two weeks and Patton didn't want any of these trucks idle. So he got us all guys that were truck drivers sitting around doing nothing to go on the *Red Ball Express* (See page 62). We used to drive twelve, fifteen hours with two drivers and we never stopped. We slept in the truck or on the ground under the truck or up in the canvas on top of the truck". Joe's truck is one of extremely few equipped with a heater. He has salvaged it from a wrecked ambulance and jerry-rigged it in his truck. "The only bad side with that," remembers Joe, "is that the commanding officers always wanted to ride with me." In November 1944, while driving somewhere around Metz, France, Joe spots a jeep with his brother Harold's regiment number. He recalls: "We spent three weekends together. I spent thanksgiving with him. He was in the Air Force and they had sent an airplane back to England and it came back with turkey and ice cream, pie... I had Thanksgiving with him while my outfit was having K-rations." This chance encounter would remain the highlight of Joe's wartime experience.

Soon after the start of the Battle of the Bulge, Joe is awoken in the middle of the night with orders to transport a truckload of paratroopers from the 82nd Airborne Division to the Ardennes. He recalls: "And we dropped them off a mile or a mile and a half from the front line and they had to walk. Snow came shortly after that. They didn't have any winter equipment, just what they brought with them." Joe witnesses the terrible cost of the war as he transports loads of frozen bodies from the Ardennes. At the end of the war, he is tasked with transporting living skeletons from the Dachau concentration camp to nearby field hospitals.

Tobacco

The toxicity of tobacco is already well established, but not widely understood or accepted. Smoking cigarettes is regarded as beneficial to fighting men. Sharing cigarettes and lighting up is an important bonding ritual that keeps hands and minds busy in periods of stress or boredom. It helps soldiers relax and steady their nerves, and many believe that it staves off hunger and combats fatigue. Some men receive as many as twenty cigarettes as part of his daily rations and more can be purchased at PX stores at the tax-exempt cost of 5¢ per pack (See page 115). Many young soldiers smoke their first cigarette during basic training and soon become addicted. In a letter to his parents dated August 11, 1944, Private John Duquoin writes: "Since we do get plenty of cigarettes, I've developed into a fairly steady smoker myself. A person practically lives on cigarettes, and when he can get it, coffee." When asked if he smoked during the war, Bill Gast of the 743rd Tank Battalion replied: "I can't remember anybody that didn't". Medics keep cigarettes in their first-aid bags because a smoke is often the first thing that a wounded man requests. John McAuliffe of the 87th Infantry Division is among a minority of soldiers who does not smoke, but he recalls being tempted: "When you're out there in the cold, you'd do anything to keep warm and smoking gave a little feeling that you were secure. I think that that's why most of them smoked." Cigarette rations are supplemented with more tobacco sent by relatives and various civic organizations doing their best to provide comfort to the soldiers. The pack of cigarettes on the right bears a tax-exempt stamp that boasts: "Good Luck and good smoking, compliments of the Red Cross". High quality American tobacco is also prized by European civilians that have been severely rationed under German occupation. It soon becomes the de facto currency on the black market. The best way to finance a good time in cities like Paris, Brussels or Liège is to bring along a few cartons of PX cigarettes. Remembers Bill Gast: "A pack of cigarettes was better than cash, it could get you just about anything."

Men of the 84th Division, in action in Belgium, are clearly relieved to receive their first cigarette rations in weeks on January 9, 1945. U.S. National Archives.

Sergeant Harry Hynes of Antlers, Oklahoma and Private Frank Benicasa of Brooklyn, New York read their mail in a barn in Rechrival, Belgium on January 9, 1945. U.S. National Archives Photo.

Mail

As the promotional matchbook to the left (A) correctly points out: "A letter from home and friends is what our boys want most". Mail call is eagerly anticipated by all the men and women serving overseas. Parents, siblings wives or girlfriends of soldiers do their best to write frequently, even when there isn't much about which to write. Betty Jane Ludwig diligently writes to her high-school sweetheart Bill Gast of the 743rd Tank Battalion. She numbers each letter and keeps track of everything she mails. The last entry in her log is Letter #448 dated September 4th, 1945. More than seventy years after the war, Betty still remembers Bill's serial number 13157568 for having written it on so many envelopes. Soldiers enjoy reading letters from home over and over again, no matter how mundane their content. Unfortunately, army rules prevent them from carrying personal letters into combat for fear that, should they be made prisoners, personal information might be used to coerce them or their relatives. In a letter to his family dated February 22, 1945, Private First Class Don Mason of the 743rd Tank Battalion writes: "We had to destroy all letters and envelopes and I always burn all mine after I answer them. I hated to at first but not anymore. It seems the best way."

People back home are eagerly awaiting news from servicemen, but for many soldiers, composing letters is daunting. Wartime cartoonist Bill Mauldin wrote: "It's very hard to compose a letter that will pass the censors when you are tired and scared and disgusted with everything that's happening.[38]"

The Army understands the crucial importance of mail as a morale booster, and does all it can to deliver it quickly and reliably, but because of the sheer volume of mail and the fluidity of troop movements, it is no simple task. An estimated five billion letters per year go to and from the armed forces during the war.

The letter addressed to Private Martin Boller at the top of this page will never be opened. It is marked with, among other things: "Deceased" and "Return to sender".

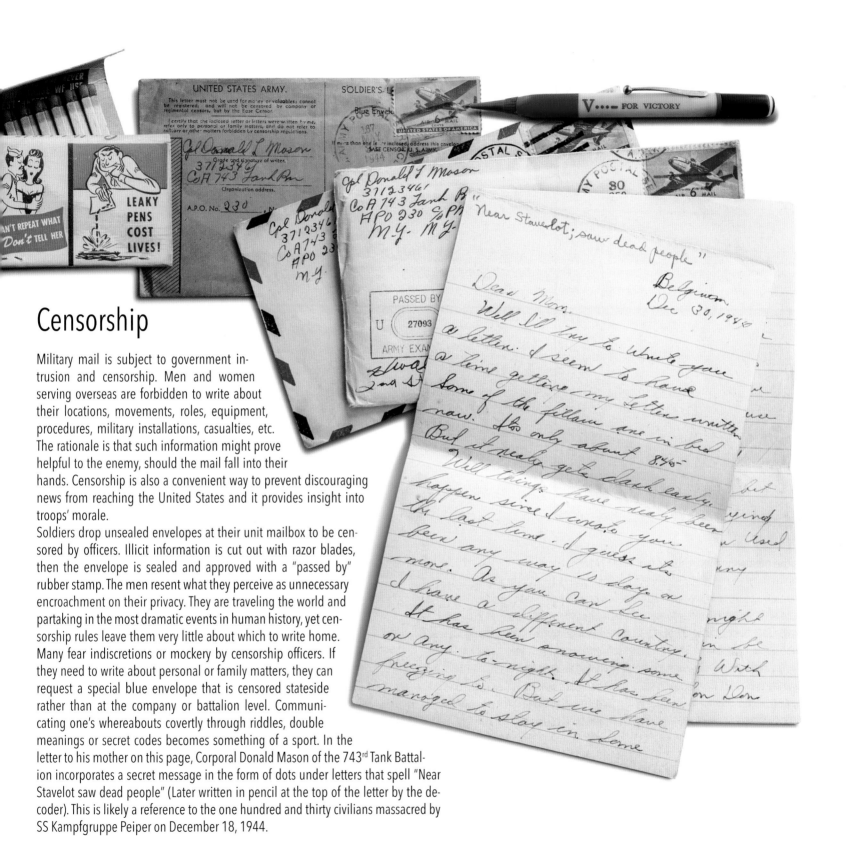

Censorship

Military mail is subject to government intrusion and censorship. Men and women serving overseas are forbidden to write about their locations, movements, roles, equipment, procedures, military installations, casualties, etc. The rationale is that such information might prove helpful to the enemy, should the mail fall into their hands. Censorship is also a convenient way to prevent discouraging news from reaching the United States and it provides insight into troops' morale.

Soldiers drop unsealed envelopes at their unit mailbox to be censored by officers. Illicit information is cut out with razor blades, then the envelope is sealed and approved with a "passed by" rubber stamp. The men resent what they perceive as unnecessary encroachment on their privacy. They are traveling the world and partaking in the most dramatic events in human history, yet censorship rules leave them very little about which to write home. Many fear indiscretions or mockery by censorship officers. If they need to write about personal or family matters, they can request a special blue envelope that is censored stateside rather than at the company or battalion level. Communicating one's whereabouts covertly through riddles, double meanings or secret codes becomes something of a sport. In the letter to his mother on this page, Corporal Donald Mason of the 743rd Tank Battalion incorporates a secret message in the form of dots under letters that spell "Near Stavelot saw dead people" (Later written in pencil at the top of the letter by the decoder). This is likely a reference to the one hundred and thirty civilians massacred by SS Kampfgruppe Peiper on December 18, 1944.

Tent and Blanket

The soldiers' standard-issue equipment includes a shelter-half (A) and one or two wool blankets (B). The shelter-half is one half of a tent consisting of a cotton duck tarp, a tent pole in three segments and five wooden pins. Two soldiers button their shelter halves together to erect a tent large enough for both of them. Shelter halves can also be used as ground cover or stretched over foxholes. In 1944, the Army starts issuing sleeping bags (C) to the general infantry. Their introduction is not so much an effort to improve the soldier's comfort, as it is a measure to save wool material which is in short supply at the time. The "fart sack" as it is known to the soldiers, is made of a washable cotton liner, a wool blanket bag and an outer water repellent cotton poplin shell. It features a quick-release zipper in case of emergency, but this does little to reassure front line troops who prefer an army blanket. Herb Adams of the 98th Parachute Infantry Division remembers: "You didn't want to be caught in the sleeping bag if there was an attack or something." Herb firmly believes that he and many soldiers like him simply could not have survived without their blankets. Soldiers dread the frigid, sixteen-hour nights of the Ardennes winter. Only when they are rotated out of combat do they get a fair crack at a decent night's sleep. The men teetering on the edge of hypothermia know that falling asleep is risky. Many have witnessed comrades freezing to death or losing limbs to frostbites. Francis Gaudere of the 119th infantry division describes a typical night: "We moved around a lot, stamped our feet and dug foxholes. A lot of us kept busy, but there are a lot of soldiers that died from the cold […] If there are any pine branches, you'd get on top trying to keep the cold off. Because there was plenty of snow and no fire, no light, nothing." Inside their foxholes, each soldier has his preferred method for wrapping, folding and tucking himself as well as he can in his clothes, blanket or sleeping bag. If several men share a foxhole, they huddle to conserve body heat. They take turns napping for an hour or two then wake up stiff, haggard and disoriented. Bill Campbell remembers waking up in his foxhole covered with snow: "Gee, I think

I'm going blind. It was snow. I was covered from head to toe with snow. Over my head and everything. Can you imagine your skin so cold it wouldn't melt snow?" Herb Adams remembers: "It was damp enough and the blanket got wet and it would freeze stiff. Now you can't fold it up."

Soldiers become exhausted to the point where they can fall asleep standing up or even walking. Herb Adams recalls: "One night, we moved fifteen miles. And we walked to the point where we were totally exhausted, because you're basically running and you'd stop for about a ten-minute break. Two or three of us would get together and lean on each other and you'd sleep a few minutes standing up. You particularly did not want to lay down in the snow."

Sergeant Harold J. Sloan of the 101st Airborne Division gathers fresh snow to melt it into drinking water on January 11, 1945 near Foy. U.S. National Archives.

Canteen

The stainless steel canteen (A) with a capacity of about a quart fits inside a cup with a folding handle (B). Both are carried on the belt in an insulated cotton and wool felt pouch (C). Herb Adams of the 82nd Airborne Division remembers that during the Battle of the Bulge, finding something to drink is a daily struggle: "Your canteen would freeze if you were out. If you were static for two days, they would try and bring up coffee for the guys and water and things of that nature. But two hours after they got there, the water froze, so what am I gonna do with it?" To melt snow or ice in their canteens, soldiers find ingenious ways to build small smokeless fires, like burning the paraffin-soaked cardboard boxes of their K-rations (See page 90). As a paratrooper, Herb is equipped with British-made Gammon bombs (D) that hold sticks of C2 explosive. This plastic composition requires a blasting cap to explode. When lit with a match, it burns slowly with an intense smokeless flame. Herb remembers: "You'd take a piece about the size of your thumbnail, you'd light that stuff and made sure the canteen had snow or something in it

otherwise you'd burn a hole right through the canteen. You'd get to the bottom of your hole and try and do that several times a day to get enough water."

The cup with the folding handle is often used to warm up water for coffee or bouillon and for heating rations. In this role, it proves more handy than the bulky meatcan (See page 84).

Halazone water purification tablets (E) are distributed to front line troops. The vial shown here is a component of the 10 in 1 ration box. Unfortunately, halazone does little to curb endemic diarrhea caused by contaminated water and the inability to properly clean canteens and utensils.

Bill walks into his local draft office on March 3, 1944, the day of his eighteenth birthday. "I signed up," remembers Bill, "and I said: 'how soon can I go?'" Bill is inducted on D-day, June 6, 1944. He recalls: "Everybody was talking about the invasion. It was a very exciting day all around. We had to take the oath that afternoon." After about ten days at Fort Devens, Bill is sent to the Infantry Replacement Training Center at Fort McClellan, Alabama. Right off the train, the training takes on a very serious tone: "They lined us up and they told us we were there to learn to kill, or we would be killed […] I took that with a grain of salt, but later on I found out how true it was." Seventeen weeks of training leave Bill in top physical condition. Most of the instructors are Southerners who seem to have inherited a grudge towards Northerners dating back to the Civil War: "They'd be up there and they'd say: 'Work the piss out of them!'"

After a brief furlough, Bill boards a Liberty ship in Brooklyn, New York. The ship transports only thirty-two officers and eighteen enlisted men, along with a cargo of foodstuff and four enormous locomotives that are welded directly to the deck for transport. The ship joins a con-

Bill upon his return to the United States after the war.

voy just as a powerful storm reaches the North Atlantic. The Liberty ship is tossed about by a forty-foot swell for two or three days. In spite of the storm and a German submarine that torpedoes one of the ships in the convoy, Bill likens the crossing to a cruise, with comfortable bunks and plentiful food, he recalls passing the time observing flying fish and dolphins leading the bow of the ship. Bill lands in Southampton, England. A week later he boards another ship bound for LeHavre, France. From there, Bill and his fellow replacements travel by train from Replacement Depot to Replacement Depot until he is finally assigned to the 28th Infantry Division and taken by truck to the front.

Bill recalls the battle of the Hurtgen Forest as the worst time in his life: "I don't think I was a religious man, but I prayed so hard to God. The artillery was so intense. That noise will be with me until I die. These shells exploded in the trees […] you were never safe." Patrols into enemy territory become routine. On a particular reconnaissance mission, Bill and his squad come within fifty feet of a German soldier in his foxhole: "We were instructed not to shoot. We're just looking and he gets out of his foxhole, he stretches, he yawns, he shook his blanket out. And I'm thinking to myself: 'Today is your lucky day!' He never saw us. At the proper time, we just left." By November 14, when the last elements of Bill's Division are finally pulled back from the bloody Hurtgen Forest, it has been reduced by almost two thirds. The 112th Regiment is sent to a quiet sector near Lieler, Luxembourg. Bill remembers: "We were like in a holding position, getting some rest and clean uniforms, showers."

The thinly spread 28th Division is hit extremely hard on the first days of the Battle of the Bulge, the fighting is savage and chaotic. The Division successively withdraws to positions near Clervaux, Salm-Chateau and Vielsalm to avoid encirclement. Along the way, Bill recalls spending a night in the basement of a house that has two inches of water on the floor and hiding among the dust-covered pews of a bombed out church with holes in the ceiling and a large crucifix tilted to one side.

Operation Greif

Devised by Adolf Hitler himself, *Operation Greif* is a key component of his Ardennes offensive. German troops in American uniforms and vehicles are to infiltrate enemy lines ahead of the Panzer divisions and secure crucial bridges before retreating Americans can demolish them. Along the way, they are to cause as much mayhem and confusion as possible through misinformation, demolition and sabotage. On October 22, 1944, Hitler assigns command of the operation to Otto Skorzeny, Germany's most illustrious SS commando. Skorzeny has distinguished himself with such spectacular operations as the rescue of Italian dictator Benito Mussolini in September 1943. Skorzeny immediately sets out to assemble and train a special brigade, but English-speaking soldiers are hard to come by, and few of them are sufficiently fluent to pass for American soldiers. Those with insufficient command of English are instructed to use such subterfuge as blurting out: "Sorry!" and running off to fake an attack of diarrhea. Gathering enough captured American uniforms, equipment and supplies also proves difficult. The meager pool of serviceable American vehicles has to be supplemented with crudely disguised German tanks. Ultimately, of Skorzeny's 2,500 men, only about 150 would impersonate American soldiers. They are hastily trained in covert operations, radio communication, demolition and sabotage. They receive courses on American mannerism, slang, and on the U.S. Army's drill, regulations, customs and command structure.

Due to delays early in the offensive, *Operation Greif's* main objective of capturing bridges over the Meuse becomes unattainable even before the operation can be launched. Consequently, Skorzeny's brigade is incorporated into other divisions. Some of his disguised commandos perform reconnaissance missions, they misdirect Allied traffic, alter road signs, cut field telephone lines and sabotage Allied equipment. After a few days, it becomes clear that the element of surprise has been lost. About a dozen of Skorzeny's men are captured, the rest abandon their American uniforms and rejoin German lines. The operation has been short-lived and its accomplishments are limited, but it sparks a paranoia among the Allies that proves even more disruptive than its stated objectives.

Word of American-clad saboteurs spreads rapidly. GIs take to testing other GIs they do not know with questions they think only a genuine American could answer: Who won the baseball World Series? What is the capital on Minnesota? Who is Rita Hayworth's husband? A wrong answer, a slight accent, or any detail that might cause suspicion are grounds for detention, or in some cases friendly fire. Pfc Paul Reed of the 17th Airborne Division recalls that General George Patton ordered that only black soldiers man traffic control points as he could be certain that there would be no black German infiltrators.[55] German prisoners wearing pieces of American uniforms they have scavenged on the battlefield are suspected of being spies and many are shot outright. Many American soldiers that have picked up German souvenirs are suspected as well. Top British General Bernard Montgomery is detained for several hours due to rumors of a German look-alike operating in the area. As a precaution, General Eisenhower is confined to his headquarters in Versailles under heavy guard.

Skorzeny's men likely knew that if captured in American uniforms, they would be shot as spies. Wilhelm Schmidt, Günther Billing and Manfred Pernass are seen here minutes before their execution by firing squad in Henri-Chapelle, Belgium on December 23, 1944. Five days earlier, the three Germans were wearing American uniforms and riding in a jeep behind American lines. They were arrested near Aywaille when they failed to give a proper password. U.S. Army photo.

On January 16, 1944, John Aguilar of the 325th Artillery Battalion braves the cold for a shampoo while his companions warm up around a fire. U.S. Army photo

Toiletries

A distinctive trait of American soldiers on furloughs is the attention they pay to their personal hygiene. While daily showers, the use of underarm deodorant (A) and preventative dental care are commonplace in America, they are still the exception in much of Europe. Each soldier arrives in Europe with a toiletry kit that includes soap (B), a toothbrush (C), tooth powder (D) or toothpaste and a shaving set (E). But the ability to use this kit usually depends on his proximity to the front lines. One can generally tell an experienced infantryman by his grease and soot-stained uniform and helmet, unshaven face and dusty hair. John McAuliffe of the 87th Infantry Division remembers that fresh off the boat, he was mistaken for a veteran because he was issued a dirty old helmet as a replacement for the one that had been stolen from him. If an infantryman has the opportunity to clean anything, he usually gives priority to his weapon. Veteran Francis Gaudere remembers: "I don't think we had a shower in three months. Every little brook we came through, we tried to wash up a little bit." Victor Sacco of the 552nd Heavy Artillery Battalion remembers: "Nobody cared, everybody smelled the same anyway." He remembers that he once had the rare privilege of visiting a mobile army shower and laundry installation: "You take all your clothes off, and you got a dog tag with a number to claim your personal things. There are hot showers and at the other end of the line, they give you all new clean clothes, except your helmet and your shoes." When Victor arrives in the town of Spa, he passes the opportunity to enjoy the world-renown curative baths because he is turned off by the sulfurous smell of the iron-rich water. Men such as artillerymen, drivers, mortar men and staff officers who tend to operate a little further back from the front lines have more frequent opportunities to wash up. They may be able to heat up water in their helmets for shaving and taking what they call a "whore's bath", washing only hands, faces and private parts.

Veteran Bill Gast of the 743rd Tank Battalion explains that to this day, seventy years after the war, he still can't take a hot shower without smiling and thinking: "Thank God, the war is over!"

The Bombing of Malmedy

In 1944, ten-year-old Philippe Krings lives in Malmedy with his widowed mother and his brother. On December 21, the town comes under German attack, but it is held by American soldiers. The Krings household is billeting twelve of these soldiers under Sergeant Joseph Corbeau. Mrs Krings provides the men with shelter, a little heat, clean laundry and a warm family atmosphere. The grateful soldiers are a reassuring presence and they gladly share their rations; Chocolate, and instant coffee are rare treats for civilians during the war. Philippe remembers the men leaving early every morning and returning late at night cold and exhausted.

On December 23, six American B-26 Marauders drop a total of eighty-six 250-pounds bombs on Malmedy by mistake. Believing he has hit the German town of Lommersum thirty miles away, the flight leader reports: "Excellent results on town." Bombs fall on either side of the Krings' home, missing it by a mere thirty feet. Windows and doors are blown in but the family is spared. Since it is no longer possible to keep the house heated, Mrs. Krings sends Philippe and his brother to the nearby house of their grandmother where a dozen people are already seeking refuge.

On Christmas Day, another sixty-four American bombs fall on Malmedy by mistake. This time, the intended target is Saint Vith, twelve miles away. The grandmother's house suffers a direct hit and collapses onto the basement where Philippe, his brother and the other refugees have gathered for safety. Alerted by Mrs Krings, Sergeant Corbeau and his men rush to the rescue. They clear some of the rubble with a bulldozer and dig the rest of their way to the basement by hand. Seven refugees are unscathed. Four, including Philippe and his brother, are seriously injured. Sergeant Corbeau commandeers a jeep to rush them through unsecured territory to a U.S. military hospital in Spa, twelve miles away. The two accidental bombings have killed more than 200 civilians and

This photo of Malmedy was taken in the summer of 1945 from one of the cathedral towers. Most of the rubble has been cleared.
Photo courtesy of Manfred Brülls.

reduced the historic center of the town to rubble. Embarrassed by this double blunder, the U.S. Army would never disclose the number of American soldiers killed by their own bombs in Malmedy.

Philippe's brother died of a crushed skull, but Philippe survived. He suffered recurring nightmares for the next fifty years. Philippe managed to gather very little information about Sergeant Corbeau who had enlisted in Cumberland, Maine in 1942, and passed away in Bryan, Ohio in 1994. To this day and in spite of exhaustive research, he has not been able to identify Sergeant Corbeau's unit or any of the other men who saved his life.

M2 Flamethrower

The flamethrower consists of twin two-gallon fuel canisters (A) pressurized by a small nitrogen tank in a backpack configuration. To fire it, the soldier first squeezes the trigger in the front (B) that actuates a revolver-style mechanism with five ignition flares (C) under the nozzle cowl. Each flare burns for about eight seconds. The soldier then squeezes the rear trigger (D) that controls the flow of pressurized napalm. The napalm is a mixture of gasoline, diesel oil and a gelling agent that produces a focused and long-burning flame. A single continuous stream empties the tanks in about eight seconds, but the flamethrower is usually fired in short bursts as the intense radiant heat quickly becomes uncomfortable to the user.

The flamethrower is particularly useful against pillboxes, bunkers and other such fortified positions. Streams of burning fuel up to 100 ft long can be poured through narrow rifle slits.

Understandably, the flamethrower has a very potent psychological effect. Chuck Wenc of the 106th Infantry Division recalls the capture of a bunker on the Siegfried line: "We had a flamethrower. We tried to squirt on the bunker. No fire, just a little 'SHHHHHH!' The door opened, and there was a white flag."

The flamethrower could be equally intimidating to the infantryman who was ordered to use it. The apparatus weighing upwards of seventy pounds made it difficult to crawl. Flamethrowers were always priority targets, and the danger of accidental burns was high. If hit by a bullet or piece of shrapnel, the pressurized fuel tanks could instantly dowse the operator and anyone near him in sticky napalm. Safety features include a shrapnel-proof flexible hose, an over-pressure release valve (E) and quick-release suspenders (F).

A team of infantrymen demonstrates the attack of a bunker during an exercise in the United States. U.S. Library of Congress photo.

Charles and Georgette Mernier Remember

In May 1940, Charles Mernier and his family flee their hometown of Bernimont, Belgium in a horse-drawn carriage to escape the German invasion of Belgium. The family finds refuge in Chablis, France. Charles' little sister is less than two days old when German bombs force the family to flee again. The newborn sister would die shortly after the Merniers' return to Belgium. Charles remembers: "There was a German in the town of Assenois that was supposed to guard the town, but we never saw him. Once in a while a German patrol would walk by. In the town, everybody had a garden, a few cows, a few sheep and chickens, so as far as food was concerned, we were doing OK." On several occasions, the family assists a local resistance network by housing escapees. Charles recalls: "Were they aviators? Or resistance fighters fleeing the Germans? I don't know. Of course my parents didn't say anything."

Charles turns ten in 1944. His father, a World War I veteran who has never fully recovered from gas poisoning, dies that same year. In September, Assenois is liberated by American soldiers. Upon hearing church bells, Charles runs to town to witness a lone Jeep with two American soldiers driving by, stopping for a while and then turning back. Stockpiles of ammunition soon spring up along country roads. Almost directly across from Charles' house are piles of shells in wooden crates guarded by black American soldiers. Charles recalls: "They broke some crates and burned them to warm up, right near the shells." Charles remembers inviting one of the soldiers to his home at the insistence of his older sister. "We did not

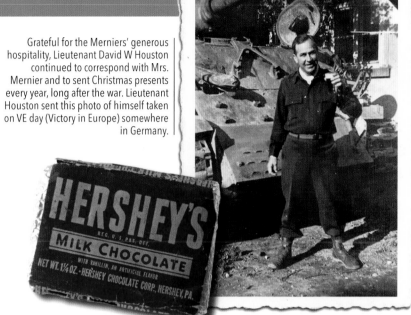

Grateful for the Merniers' generous hospitality, Lieutenant David W Houston continued to correspond with Mrs. Mernier and to sent Christmas presents every year, long after the war. Lieutenant Houston sent this photo of himself taken on VE day (Victory in Europe) somewhere in Germany.

understand each other," recalls Charles, "he came home, we gave him something to eat, then he left." During the Battle of the Bulge, Charles watches large formations of American C-47 Skytrain planes flying towards Bastogne. The large and comfortable Mernier home is selected to billet American officers as they pass through Assenois. On December 28, Lieutenant David Houston arrives along with staff officers of the 68th Tank Battalion. That evening, Mrs. Mernier prepares a special meal for the soldiers, and although they have some difficulty communicating, the atmosphere is congenial. Charles is particularly impressed by a certain Captain Parker, a tall, handsome man who carries two pearl-handle pistols like a cowboy. The December 28 entry in Lieutenant Houston's journal reads: "Moved to Assenois, Belgium. Staying in the house of a very nice widow with four children. They are very nice and very good to us all. They shared their beer, sausage and other food with us. We gave them coffee and bread and cheese." The following day he wrote: "Still in Assenois and the people are really treating us swell. Wish we could reciprocate."

Georgette Mernier is born Georgette Gadisseur in 1938 in Seraing, Belgium. Her father George Gadisseur is a member of a resistance network. He became famous for his daring escape from a German prison and his escapade across Europe. Due to Georgette's young age at the time, her souvenirs of the war are few, but remain vivid. She recalls the convoy of American vehicles that liberated her hometown: "We were standing on the sidewalk and soldiers were throwing chocolate and candy. The famous chocolate! I would not have traded it for anything in the world! The wonderful aroma of that chocolate! I can still taste it!" Georgette's cousin, an attractive sixteen-year-old girl, lives with Georgette's family. She goes on a few dates with young American soldiers and Georgette is sent along as a chaperone. Georgette remembers a particular soldier who befriended her. "I was his favorite!" recalls Georgette. "Before he left, he gave me a rosary that I kept to this day." Georgette believes that the soldier later died in Bastogne, the city where she and Charles now live.

Charles and Georgette are the parents of organist and composer Benoît Mernier.

The Medical Corps

Every soldier is equipped with a first aid kit (A) that contains a sterile bandage known as a Carlisle dressing. Early in the war, the bandage is encased in a hermetically sealed brass (B) or tin shell to protect it from contamination. To save money and metal, the packaging is eventually replaced with an airtight paper laminate (C). Starting in 1941, the Carlisle dressing is supplemented with a small packet of sulfanilamide powder (D) that the soldiers are to sprinkle over open wounds. "Sulfa" also came in tablet form (E) as it is the first antibacterial drug that can be taken internally. Sulfa significantly reduces the chance of infection and it shores up the morale of wounded soldiers by giving them a sense of control in very traumatic situations. The airborne version of the first aid kit (F) comes in a hermetically sealed pouch of rubberized fabric that must be torn open. Because airborne troops typically operate out of the reach of the medical corps, their kit is supplemented with a morphine syrette (G) and a tourniquet.

The medical care of soldiers is organized in tiers from the aidman providing first aid in the field, to aid stations, clearing stations, field hospitals and general hospitals. Each level provides progressively more advanced and specialized care further away from the front. At each step, patients are either returned to duty, or moved up to the next level for further treatment. At peak strengths in 1944, the medical department of the U.S. Army includes 700,000 military personnel, about 8.5 percent of the Army. [58]

At least one aid-man is embedded in each company. He is trained as a medical or surgical technician and tasked with providing first aid on the battlefield. His job in combat typically consists in controlling hemorrhages, dressing wounds, wrapping men in blankets and injecting morphine to control pain and shock. He is often required to take enormous risks to reach wounded men and his work is complicated by the cold that numbs fingers and freezes morphine and plasma. Richard Roush, a medic with the 84th Infantry Division wrote: "It didn't really make much difference whether a soldier was barely or severely wounded in the extremely cold weather he would immediately go into shock. We couldn't do anything for him because we didn't have any means to warm a wounded soldier. [59]" In many tragic instances, all an aid man can do is provide the last measure of comfort to dying men in the form of reassuring words, sips of water and cigarettes.

The role of the aid man is not limited to the battlefield. Famous cartoonist and veteran Bill Mauldin wrote: "The aid man is the dogface's family doctor, and he is regarded as an authority on every minor ailment from a blister to a cold in the head. The aid man usually takes this responsibility quite seriously. He lances and patches blisters with all the professional pride of a brain specialist removing a tumor. [38]"

Litter bearers are usually dispatched by jeeps in teams of two or four and tasked with rushing casualties back to forward aid stations. Their work is physically demanding and equally perilous as that of the aid-man. The forward aid station is usually located within a few miles of the front in tents or suitable buildings. It is minimally equipped and staffed with aid men and physicians. War correspondent Ernie Pyle wrote: "The station can knock down, move, and set up again in an incredibly short time. They are as proficient as a circus.[32]" The wounded are triaged, warmed up when possible and stabilized with plasma and morphine as needed. Their dressings are not usually replaced but rather reinforced as removing a dressing risks restarting or aggravating hemorrhages. Frostbite and psychiatric casualties are common, but the majority of wounds are caused by artillery shell fragments. The patient's wounds are debrided and cleaned. Surgeons have discovered that to lessen the chances of post-operative infections or gangrene, it is best to leave bandaged wounds temporarily open, and suture them at a later date. Ralph Storm, a Red Cross medic wrote: "These facilities were near the front and provided only patch-up work for the wounded. The goal was to keep patients alive and send them on to the next hospital where more sophisticated procedures could be used. The general hospitals where the patients could be reconstructed and rehabilitated were located in areas more distant from the front in such continental cities as Liège, Paris, Dijon, and many cities and towns in England.[60]"

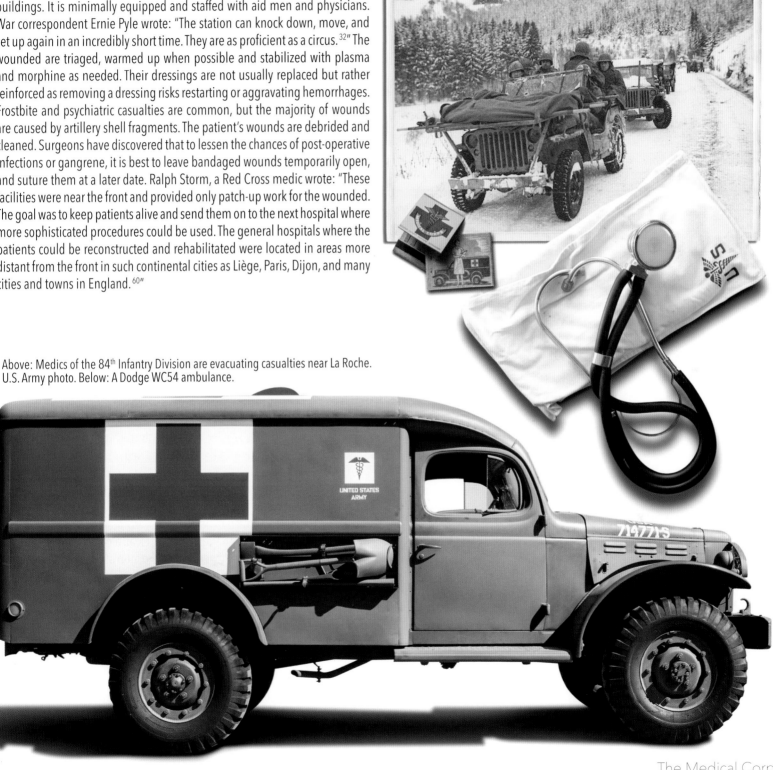

Above: Medics of the 84th Infantry Division are evacuating casualties near La Roche. U.S. Army photo. Below: A Dodge WC54 ambulance.

V-Mail

Victory mail or V-Mail is a microfilm-based airmail system put in place to streamline the enormous volume of correspondence to and from military personnel overseas. V-mail is written on letter-size, single-side forms designed to be folded and sealed without the need for an envelope. From post offices, V-mail forms are diverted to facilities where they are sorted, opened, censored and photographically reduced onto rolls of 16mm microfilm. A 5.5-ounce roll of film holds up to 1,700 letters, the equivalent of about 50 pounds of standard mail. The microfilm is flown overseas, enlarged onto black and white photographic paper about one quarter the size of the original forms and re-integrated into the postal service. A system of tracking numbers ensures that each roll of film has safely reached its destination before the original forms are discarded. V-mail is free to military personnel. It requires 3¢ stamps from civilians; the same cost as regular letters, but half the price of Airmail. Transit time is one to two weeks for V-mail (the same as Airmail), and four to six weeks for regular mail.

Medic Kit

Medics wear the red cross armbands (A) that identifies them as neutral and unarmed and that, in theory, provides protection under the Geneva Convention. Red crosses on the helmets (B) are generally painted by the medics themselves without official specifications. Medics carry two side bags (C) that hold a variety of supplies including medical record tags (D) that they attach to each casualty, tourniquets (E), shatter-proof pill containers, and adhesive bandages (F), sterile dressings (G), morphine syrettes (I) and scissors (H) to cut away clothing. In addition to critical emergency care, medics also do their best to provide emotional support and what little comfort they can. Water and cigarettes (J) are among the things that wounded and dying men requested most.

Dorothy Barre is born Dorothy Taft on July 17, 1918 in Oxford, Massachusetts. She is a nursing student at the Massachusetts Memorial Hospital in Boston when Hitler declares war on the United States. Dorothy remembers: "Almost everybody that was in my class had already joined the service. […] When I came home from training I got work. One case, a little girl in a coma, was about ten years old and she died. Then there was an elderly woman that had a stroke, then I thought I'm not gonna do that for the rest of my life." When Dorothy joins the Army in July of 1943, she is assigned to the 16th General Hospital. The most vivid memories of her basic training at Fort Devens, Massachusetts include crawling under live machine gun fire, and a gas mask drill in a gas chamber. She also recalls: "All kinds of marching and many courses including one titled *Kill or be killed*." On December 29, 1943, she boards a ship in Boston and arrives

Left photo: Dorothy with two of her fellow nurses: Lieutenant Darcy Lawlor and Lieutenant Ann Nigro in Jupille, Belgium.

in Liverpool, England ten days later. For the next eight months, she cares for American soldiers stationed in Great Britain. Dorothy follows the 16th General Hospital to Normandy, France. She spends her first night in France sleeping under the stars in a pasture. In October 1944, the 16th General Hospital relocates to Belgium. Dorothy and her fellow nurses are temporarily billeted in a bank building overlooking the Avroy Boulevard in Liège before they settled more permanently in the castle of Fayembois, nearer to the General Hospital in Jupille. "They just took a big field," recalls Dorothy, "And the guys put the tents up so each tent had thirty patients in it, and then there was a building for the operating room, it was more like a shack." There are enough tents to accommodate 1,000 patients, but without electricity or running water. Each tent is heated with a small potbellied stove. The nurses work by the light of kerosene lanterns and flashlights.

To face the onslaught of casualties during the Battle of the Bulge, the 16th General Hospital temporarily serves as an evacuation hospital, treating only the most urgent cases and preparing all others for evacuation to Paris or Great Britain. Dorothy works twelve-hour shifts, seven days a week. Soldiers arrive straight from the front, wrapped in Army blankets. Dorothy remembers: "We just washed them up, got johnnies on them. […] I carried codeine aspirin around the clock, if they needed morphine, I went to the medicine tent and got that. […] Just gave it if we thought they needed it. We reinforced their dressings, not usually changed them. Then we got them hot meals, because a lot of them had not eaten in days. They were worn out, they were exhausted, they looked like old men." Most patients are evacuated within twenty-four hours to make room for the continuous flow of new arrivals and so, remembers Dorothy: "We never got to know them." On occasion, the field hospital also admits Belgian civilians, primarily the victims of some 2,141 V1 flying bombs that fall on or around Liège. Dorothy vividly remembers a young girl dying from shrapnel wounds with her mother sitting by her side.

Underwear

The wool and cotton undershirt and long drawers play important roles in fighting the cold, but the inability to wash clothing takes a toll on the soldiers. Pfc Donald Schoo of the 80th Infantry Division wrote: "You are thirsty, tired, have diarrhea, your feet are sore, you are dirty, itchy and you stink. You hurt all over and chafe.[62]" Some units are lucky enough to receive new underwear or socks once in a while; these are generally distributed along with rations or mail. Lynn Aas of the 17th Airborne Division wrote: "About every two weeks we received new underwear. Because it was so cold we merely put the new ones on the inside. At one time I had three pairs of long underwear and two pairs of trousers on to keep warm.[63]" Richard Stone of the 526th Armored Infantry Battalion recalls that his company was issued white long underwear and white towels to wear over their uniforms as snow camouflage.[64]

M24 "Chaffee" Light Tank

The M24 is designed to succeed the obsolete M5 Stuart tank (See page 39). Among the major improvements are a more powerful 75mm main gun, improved suspension, longer track for better off-road capabilities. The armor is only an inch thick, but long glacis slopes on both the crew compartment and the turret are designed to deflect rather than stop incoming shells. In addition to the main gun, the M24 is armed with a turret-mounted .50 Browning machine gun and two .30 Browning machine guns, one coaxial with the main gun and one in a ball mount for use by the assistant driver. The M24 is crewed by five men: A commander, a driver, an assistant driver, a gunner and a loader. The first thirty-four M24 arrive in Europe just in time to be rushed into the Battle of the Bulge.

This tank of the 18th Cavalry Reconnaissance Squadron was photographed in Petit-Thier in February 1945. U.S. Army photo.

Automatic Pistol M1911A1

The M1911 Pistol is yet another classic design of prolific firearm designer John Browning who also developed the Browning automatic rifle (See page39) and the M1917-19 Browning machine guns (See page 30). With only minor upgrades, the M1911 would remain the standard-issue sidearm of the United States Army until the 1980s. The M1911 is a .45 caliber, recoil operated semi-automatic pistol fed by a seven-round straight magazine inserted in the Grip. The pistol is commonly known as the Colt .45 (although it is produced by other manufacturers as well) or simply as the .45. It is primarily issued to officers or to tank crews and other men who work in tight spaces or carry heavy loads such as radio operators, machine gunner, etc. By the end of the war, more than 2.5 million M1911 pistols have been manufactured.

Lighting

Late December in the Ardennes sees as little as eight hours of daylight per day. Much of the Battle of the Bulge is fought in the dark, which plays up the fears of the soldiers and further adds to their discomfort. Near the front lines, any sort of flame or light is strictly forbidden. Even the glow of a cigarette can be seen from great distances and risks drawing enemy fire. Army-issued flashlights (A) are restricted to few men to limit the potential for careless use. Dr. John MacAuliffe of the 87th Infantry Division remembers that during his night guard watches he had to carefully cloak himself under a rain jacket before he could strike a match to read the time on his watch. Those who give into the temptation of tobacco, often do so in defiance of orders and have to be equally careful. Peter Drevinski of the 26th Infantry Division remembers that smoking a pipe afforded certain advantages: Pipes are more discreet since the glow of the tobacco is hidden within the bowl and the pipe can be used to warm one's hands. Even the men in the rear have to abide by strict blackout rules. German light observation planes often patrol at night. Donald Bein of the 9th Armored Division wrote: "Every night about 10-11 pm, we called him *Bed Check Charlie*. He was looking for lights and any info that would help the German cause. He flew without any lights at all, and was at a low altitude."

Finding a reliable source of light to work, read, write or otherwise pass long evenings is often problematic since war-ravaged towns are usually without electricity. Soldiers are always on the lookout for candles (B) in vacant houses and churches. Flat candles with broad wicks (C) are sometimes distributed for heating rations. In the frigid foxholes, even a candle is a welcome source of heat. Henry Mooseker of the 87th Infantry Division recalls: "I would gouge out a shelf in the fox hole side for my paraffin candle. I'd insert the candle, light it and have some warmth.47" Chester Wenc of the 106th Infantry Division remembers that soldiers improvised a sooty, but effective sort of oil lamp by inserting a shoelace into a bottle of Army-issued "bug juice", an oil-based insect repellent (D).

Chow

If it does not always succeed, the War Department goes to great length to provide soldiers everywhere with nourishing, balanced and palatable food. In garrisoned areas, units are sometimes alloted money with which to purchase fresh provisions from local sources. In combat zones, they are provided with non-perishable bulk food. Staples include dehydrated vegetables and mashed potatoes, powdered eggs and milk, pasta, canned fruit, frozen, canned or cured meat such as bacon, sausage, hot dogs, chipped beef, Spam, etc. There is usually one mess detail per company with a kitchen truck, driver and several cooks and bakers. The kitchen truck is a two-and-a-half-ton truck, sometimes towing a trailer or a water tank. It transports an icebox, two or three M-1937 field ranges and a full complement of baking trays, stockpots, and utensils. Field ranges are fired with pressurized gasoline burners and can be configured as cook tops, ovens or griddles.

Marcel Schmetz is twelve years old when a field kitchen of the 1st Infantry Division sets up shop at his family's farm in Clermont, Belgium. He is proud to help the cooks pump up the pressurized gasoline burners every day. He recalls that the food was delicious and plentiful and that his family was always served first: "We

had not eaten this well in a very long time! We had good cooks, they served steaks, and sausages and we ate all we wanted!" Marcel remembers that after each meal, the cooks throw away enormous quantities of leftovers. So much, that the family's pigs become sick from over-eating.

Wherever possible, kitchens are set up in buildings, usually near the regimental or battalion bivouac area, but they sometimes operate out of tents, or even in the back of the kitchen trucks. Each soldier carries his own mess kit that included a lidded meat can (AKA shit-skillet), a knife, fork and spoon. The meat can and its lid can be threaded together to form a three-compartment tray. The soldiers form a chow line and are served as they file past the cooks.

The quality of the food varies greatly depending on the skill of the cook and the supplies at hand. 1st Lt Wesley Ross of the 146th Engineer Combat Battalion wrote: "Breakfast might include stewed prunes, oatmeal with reconstituted dried milk, scrambled powdered eggs, bacon, and toast with jam. It did not look too appetizing when so intermingled, but it tasted better than it looked, and it had a definite edge over those gruesome K-rations. Also, having the food piled together helped to keep it warm. Our cooks were artists in their ability to take smelly powdered eggs and powdered milk and turn them into something reasonably palatable.[4]"

In spite of the cooks' best efforts, many soldiers grow bored with army meals. Sgt Henry Mooseker of the 87th Infantry Division wrote: "We searched every beat up house, hovel, cellar and barn for anything edible. I can remember finding Brussels sprouts, carrots and some potatoes in a root cellar. I found a can of fat that most houses stored and used to fry the potatoes. […] Disregarding standing orders not to eat or drink things we found, we gobbled up anything edible. A good find was fruit and jelly preserves.[67]"

Because locals have been barred from hunting under German occupation, wild game is abundant in the Ardennes. There are also plenty of farm animals roaming free because pens or fences have been blown open by shells or torn

Albert Hiesic and Camden Sargent of the 486th Antiaircraft Artillery Battalion seem oblivious to the sleet as they eat their chow in Trou-Du-Bois, Belgium, January 4, 1945. U.S. Army photo.

by passing tanks. Wesley Ross of the 146th Combat Engineer Battalion wrote: "Christmas Day 1944, a doe and a yearling crossed in front of our truck. We stopped and I told the men in back to shoot her. After ten or more rounds had been fired, I yelled: 'Cease fire!' […] The doe then wandered back across the road, so I shot her. There was a single hole in her hide – another indication of superb American marksmanship! The fresh meat was a welcome change from our recent diet. Several weeks previously, B Company's various work parties returned to the company bivouac area one evening with five hogs, two cows, and a deer. […] The animals were a nuisance around minefields, walking into the trip wires, detonating the mines and killing themselves in the process.[4]"

During combat, every attempt is made to deliver at least one hot meal per day to the men on the front line, preferably under cover of darkness. The food is transported by jeep in insulated aluminum containers, or the kitchen trucks themselves deliver the food that is prepared on board. John McAuliffe of the 87th Infantry Division recalls: "They had big cauldrons of coffee and maybe a big tray of oatmeal, something like that. And they would leave you this K-ration for your noon meal. And if possible, they would come up again at night with the truck and give you some Spam or something like that."

Frank Mareska of the 75th Infantry Division wrote: "Men wolfed down their food in any sequence: whether they ate ass backwards or whatever! Dessert followed by the main dish. The important thing was not to drop anything or waste anything! Everything went! We used dirt, fallen snow, and leaves to clean our mess gear.[28]"

During combat operations, a good many men are out of reach of the mess crews. They have to rely on processed food rations, either individual rations such as the K or C rations (See pages 88 & 90)), or collective rations such as the 10 in 1. The 10 in 1 ration box contains much the same type of bulk foodstuff available to the kitchen trucks, but in quantities sufficient for 10 men for 1 day. It is subdivided into four smaller boxes, each containing one half of five rations. The box shown on the opposite page is marked as the second half of 5 rations. It contains the heavier components such as cans of meat, fruits, vegetables, jams, etc. The first half of 5 rations box contains dry components such as breakfast cereal, individual lunch packets, crackers, powdered beverages, sugar, confections, cigarettes, matches, toilet paper, etc. The 10 in 1 ration is meant to be prepared collectively, but no specific provision is made to supply the men with cooking pots and utensils, forcing them to make do with what they find. Compact gasoline stoves are available, but in limited quantities. Frank Mareska of the 75th infantry Division wrote that though they are referred to as "Squad Stoves", they are not nearly that widespread: "One stove was issued to each platoon! Thus in lieu of one stove for twelve men, we had one stove for forty men. Getting some hot water anytime of day was a long drawn out affair. Often, men drank their instant as ice coffee or ice tea or what have you.[28]"

A Nasty Case of "GI"

In addition to the cold, fear and other miseries of war, the men have to contend with endemic diarrhea brought on by deficient sanitation, stress, lack of sleep and erratic consumption of concentrated food. Aware of the irony, GIs refer to diarrhea as the GI, short for gastrointestinal. Most men wear as much clothing as they can to combat the cold, but explosive diarrhea and multiple layers of pants and underwear with button flies is a recipe for disaster. Robert Kauffman of the 3rd Armored Division wrote: "I felt a sudden discomfort come over me. And then, just as quickly, I was seized with fiery convulsions in my lower abdominal region. All of a sudden the whole scene became clear; along with my comrades, I had been smitten with what each of us must have been convinced was terminal diarrhea. […] Knowing that I was entrapped inside the webbing and straps of my combat harness, and also knowing that it would take superhuman effort to extricate myself quickly from all that paraphernalia, there was but one thing to do and that was to become momentarily hysterical.[68]"

To compound the indignity, sufferers typically lack any privacy or the means to wash themselves or change clothing. They are left drained of energy, humiliated and thoroughly disgusted. They have no choice but to continue wearing soiled clothing for days or weeks.

Paul Fussell of the 103rd Infantry Division wrote: "One day, I was marching toward a town where we were billeted. Suddenly, with no warning at all, my stomach churned and terrible cramps forced out a cascade of liquid shit before I could scuttle to the side of the road and drop my trousers. While the company marched stolidly on, I spent fifteen minutes in a rutabaga patch trying to clean myself up.[16]" Fussell cut off his soaked long underwear with his trench knife and attempted, with little success, to wipe himself with the only paper he had: fancy stationery and pages from a Field Message Book.

Marcel Schmetz Remembers

Marcel is seven years old at the start of the war. He lives in a farm in Clermont with his parents and his brother Henri. Marcel will always remember the morning of May 10, 1940, because his mother was crying as she woke him up. She told him: "You are not going to school today. The Germans have attacked Belgium. Your dad is coming to kiss you goodbye before he goes to war." Part of Clermont and a dozen other border towns are annexed to Germany. Soon, Marcel and his schoolmates are made to give the Hitler salute every day and speak German in class, under threat of deportation. As new German citizens, the inhabitants of his town are not rationed quite as severely as those of occupied Belgium, but some products are nonetheless impossible to procure. People make their own soap by boiling Ivy leaves. They substitute coffee with roasted grain or chicory roots. Children receive only one bar of chocolate per year as a Christmas gift from Adolf Hitler. Marcel walks to school in wooden clogs as leather shoes are no longer available. Worn out bicycle tires are replaced with sections of old rubber hoses. All the farm produce is to be sold to Germany at low regulated prices. But, recalls Marcel: "In a farm, you always found enough food to eat, one way or the other."

Right: Twelve-year-old Marcel Schmetz in 1945. Bottom: Marcel and his wife Mathilde (affectionately known as M&M) are world-renowned for their museum in Thimister-Clermont, and for the warm hospitality they have extended to hundreds of veterans and their families, going so far as to house and transport them free of charge.

In 1943, at the age of 17, Marcel's brother Henri is conscripted into the German Army, but rather than joining, he goes into hiding. On the second floor of the house, inside a double brick wall, there is a small secret space, which can be accessed through a trap door in the attic. For fifteen months, Henri lives upstairs, never leaving the house, ready to vanish into his hiding place at the least sign of trouble, an ordeal that would leave him psychologically damaged for life.

An other unforgettable date for Marcel is September 11, 1944, the day the Americans liberate his town. Two older German soldiers are digging a trench nearby. Hungry and disillusioned, they beg for food, explaining that they have lost the war and that Hitler is mad. Marcel recalls: "We gave them sandwiches, they thanked us and they jumped into their truck. They were leaving on one side of the house as the Americans were arriving on the other. When we saw the first American vehicles, we were overjoyed! People were crying with joy!" He remembers tanks driving cross-country, ripping through barb wire fences, jeeps and columns of GIs walking by, rifles at the ready: "We welcomed them as we could, but we did not speak English, and they did not stop. The next morning, support troops arrived with all the equipment. They set up cannons in the fields."

At the end of November, Marcel's family farm billets one hundred and ten soldiers from the 1st Infantry Division. Aside from a single room reserved for the family, there is hardly a square foot of space in the house, attic and hay barn that is not taken by a soldier's bedroll. Three field kitchen stoves are set up to feed the soldiers housed at the Schmetz's and other neighboring farms. Marcel is proud to help the army cooks pump up the stoves' pressurized gasoline tanks. He and his family are always served first at the chow line, and the food is good and plentiful. Soldiers leave precipitously about two weeks later at the start of the Battle of the Bulge, but not without leaving entire boxes of canned food, rations and chocolate bars. Marcel recalls that the family would still be eating American food several years after the war, and to this day, he maintains the habit of eating a half bar of chocolate for breakfast every morning.

M10 Tank Destroyer

Soldiers refer to M10 tank destroyers as "TDs". The M10 and the Sherman tanks are built on the same chassis and share many characteristics. They are designed to be compact and relatively lightweight so as to be easily shipped overseas. In theory, they make up for their thin armor with speed, range and maneuverability - The M10 can achieve speeds in excess of 30 miles per hour and a range of about 180 miles. The low profile, open-top pentagonal turret with large counterweights in the back lend the M10 its characteristic angular profile. The TD is armed with a 3" gun and a Browning .50 caliber machine gun can be mounted on the turret. It is crewed by five men: The commander and driver sit in front and three gunners man the gun turret. The open top, which can be covered with a waterproof canvas tarp, leaves the gunners vulnerable to air bursts, mortar rounds and snipers, but it allows for quick escapes, and it provides very good

visibility. With all three gunners enjoying 360° views of their surroundings, the M10 is very good as spotting potential targets, but slow at acquiring them: The hand-cranked turret takes a full minute to rotate 180°.

These two TDs were photographed by the light of their gunfire in the Vosges on January 25, 1945. U.S. Army photo.

Field Rations, Types C & D

A C rations comes packed in two tin cans. The so-called bread can (A) holds combinations of biscuits (C), compressed breakfast cereals, soluble coffee (D), chocolate, hard candy (E), caramels, jam, sugar (F), etc. Edward Filush of the 94th Infantry Division describes the meat portion of the ration (B) as: "A soup-can-sized main dish of stew or dog food or something similar.[69]" Joe Landry, a truck driver of the 776th Anti Aircraft Artillery Battalion remembers: "One of them was beans and franks. We used to punch a hole in it, and put it on the manifold of the truck. We would drive and it would heat up." A day's supply of C rations is sometimes supplemented with an accessory packet (G) that includes cigarettes, matches (H), toilet paper (I) and chewing gum (J). The Field ration D (K) is a pocket-size, chocolate-based emergency ration conditioned in a paraffin-dipped cardboard box. With the addition of oat flour and other ingredients, the Army makes sure that the bar resists melting and that it is not too palatable, for fear that it might be consumed as a tasty snack rather than an emergency ration. The D ration is notoriously hard on the stomach. Instructions on the box warn: "To be eaten slowly (in about a half hour)".

A Segregated Army

In deference to the Jim Crowe laws of southern states, the US Army is racially segregated. Black servicemen are directed to all-black divisions. The facilities in which they train and live are often inferior to those afforded to white units. When Harold Ward volunteers for the Navy in January of 1940, he is sent to the Naval Station in Norfolk Virginia where four old World War I barracks known as Unit B-east are reserved for black recruits and separated by a 10-foot chain link fence. The fact that he is not initially trained as a sailor comes as a shock to Harold. He recalls: "We were servants, that was our duty. I stayed angry through the whole damned war.[…] We were trained to set a table, make a bed, shine a shoe. I was forced to serve the war as a flunky!"

A widespread prejudice of the time holds that black men lack the grit and intelligence to make good soldiers. Consequently, a good portion of black recruits are restricted to non-combatant duties. They are tasked with the same sort of unqualified manual labor that is often their lot in civilian life. They serve food, dig ditches, latrines and graves, drive and unload trucks, wash laundry, etc. Most are only summarily trained in the use of weapons; many are disgusted to find out that even German prisoners of war are treated better than they are. As Corporal Rupert Trimmingham and eight other black men of the Army Corps of Engineers travel through a small town in central Louisiana, they find out that only the train station lunchroom would serve black men, and only if they enter through the back door and eat in the kitchen. From the kitchen, they observe two dozen German prisoners of war and their guards. Trimmingham wrote: "They entered the lunchroom, sat at the tables, had their meals served, talked, smoked, in fact had quite a swell time.[70]"

In Europe, the U.S. Army's segregation policies are at odds with local laws. There are no restrictions on black soldiers using any public facility, or visiting the bars, restaurants or movie theaters of their choices. This causes resentment among white soldiers from Southern States. While stationed in England, Michael Bilder of the 5th Infantry Division visits the town of Andover on weekend passes. He wrote: "The girls in Andover and all over the UK danced and dated black and white soldiers alike. Some of the southerners in our outfit asked the girls why they danced with Negro soldiers. 'They told us they were American Indians,' was the reply. That must have been the excuse that some of the guys were waiting for because they came back to Andover the following weekend armed for bear. […] At first it was almost comical, like something out of a Chaplin movie. If things had stayed that way, everyone might have walked away with nothing more than cuts and bruise. Then we heard shots ring out. We dove for cover. This had now gone way beyond what almost anybody wanted.[71]" Bilder recalls that according to rumors, twenty soldiers died in the melee that day, most of them black.

All-black companies serve in every branch of the army and fight with distinction. Among them are the famous 332nd Fighter Group, better known as the Tuskegee Airmen, the 333rd Field Artillery which is attached to the 101st Airborne Division during the siege of Bastogne, and the 761st "Black Panthers" Tank Battalion that was welcomed to Europe by General Patton's famous words:" I don't care what color you are as long as you go up there and kill those Kraut sonsobitches.[72]"

In the chaos that characterizes the start of the Battle of the Bulge, black and white soldiers find themselves fighting side by side. Support troops like cooks and truck drivers, many of them black, are handed rifles and thrown into the fight. There is no time for racism in the heat of battle and many white soldiers have their first opportunity to see for themselves just how unfounded their prejudices had been. 1st Lt Gus Blass of the 4th Cavalry Group wrote: "There were many heroes among those black fellows driving, hauling and fighting. At St. Vith, they got out of their trucks and fought side-by-side with us.[73]" Severe losses in the Ardennes cause an acute shortage of infantrymen. Colonel John Lee, the head of the Army Service of Supplies, proposes that black support personnel be allowed to volunteer for front line duty and assigned as replacements in white units. General Eisenhower approved the idea with the condition that they be integrated as all-black platoons, rather than individually. Thousands of black servicemen step forward. In one engineer outfit, 171 out of 186 men volunteer, as do 100 men from a 260-men Quartermaster Laundry Company. Enough men volunteer to form fifty-three all-black riflemen platoons, thirty-seven of which are integrated in white companies.[74] This modest first step towards integration and the distinguished record of black companies in World War II would eventually lead to the full desegregation of the armed forces by President Harry Truman in 1948.

Corporal Carlton Chapman was a member of the famous 761st Armored Battalion nicknamed "Black Panthers". U.S. Library of Congress photo.

Field Rations, Type K

To feed individual soldiers where delivering fresh meals is impossible or too dangerous, the Quartermaster Corps provides pocket-size processed food meals designated field rations, type K. The composition of these meals has been the object of considerable research and testing. K rations have to be compact, palatable and provide about 3000 calories per day, good nutrition and a long shelf life. A day's worth of food comes in three cardboard boxes marked "Breakfast", "Dinner" or "Supper". The food consists of a canned meat, cheese or egg entrée (A) and a cellophane packet with various combinations of concentrated foodstuff such as dry biscuits (B), crackers, instant coffee (C), powdered fruit beverages, bouillon powder, sugar, hard candy, caramels, chocolate, chewing gum (D), fruit bars, etc. Over time, K rations are improved with more variety and supplemented with comfort items such as cigarettes (E), matches (F), toilet paper (G), and disposable wooden spoons (H).

K rations are not intended to be consumed for more than a few consecutive days, but they are sometimes distributed for weeks on end. In 1944, the army procures more than 105 million rations.[75] Soldiers often feel that K rations are issued not out of necessity, but rather as a cop-out. They complain that biscuits become stale in old or improperly stored K rations, and that mint flavor from the chewing gum pervades the entire ration.[76] The powdered lemonade is so tart and unnatural that soldiers refer to it as "battery acid". Lt. David Kregg of the 84th Infantry Division recalls that the lunch rations usually included a can of cheese that felt like a rock in your stomach. Therefore the men preferred to eat the breakfast and lunch

A man of the 393rd Infantry Regiment protect the muzzle of his rifle with a ration box. U.S. Army photo.

rations first and only ate the dinner rations when they had nothing else.[77]

When over-consumed, K rations become monotonous. They fail to deliver sufficient energy and nutrients, in part because the men tend to discard items they do not like, keeping only confections, coffee and cigarettes. Veteran Francis Gaudere remembers: "A couple of times, we really got sore. Somebody back there took the coffee out of the breakfast rations. We had no coffee for a few days."

To make the K rations resistant to the rigors of combat and the outdoors, they are double-boxed in cardboard. Starting in 1943, plain black print on the outer box is replaced with bold, colorful graphics to make the rations easier to select and more appealing. The inner boxes are dipped in paraffin wax for protection against moisture, bugs and contamination. Incidentally the paraffin-soaked cardboard burns like a candle and gives off little smoke. Soldiers use them to thaw their frozen canteens, to warm up their hands, or the ration itself. Bill Campbell of the 28th Infantry Division remembers that the men skewered the cans at the tip of their bayonets to hold them over the flame. Oftentimes, soldiers have no choice but to eat the rations cold, if not frozen. Reuel Long of the 90th Infantry Division recalls that he kept his breakfast ration under his armpit to keep it from freezing overnight.[78]

Left : Charlie Warren and Victor Sacco in the Hurtgen forest in the fall of 1944.
Right : Victor somewhere in Belgium.

The observation post rarely stays in one place for more than two or three days, and Victor is rarely told where he is or where he will be moving next. He nonetheless remembers place names like Stavelot, Malmedy and Spa and a stay in the picturesque castle of Froidcourt in Stoumont. Victor recalls pulling guard duty and patrolling the grounds in the bitter cold. Etched in his mind are French words scribbled on the wall of an improvised jail cell in the basement: "Perdu dans les bois" (Lost in the woods). Every night, a small German plane flies over the castle. "They shot at him first, but he wasn't dropping any bombs" recalls Victor, "and before you know, everybody was waving at him and he was waving back."

Victor Sacco is born in Worcester, Massachusetts on February 24, 1923. He is drafted into the Armed Forces in the summer of 1943. Victor chooses the Infantry when he finds out that it offers a longer furlough after basic training than other branches of service. "They put us on a train to South Carolina." remembers Victor, "We were supposed to go to Infantry. They stopped the train and sent us back to Fort Bragg because they needed men for the artillery. And that's how we got in the Artillery."

Victor recalls: "Barely six months after we started training, we were on a ship heading for England. We sailed April 6, 1944 from New York harbor on the British ship Aquitania." Victor is part of the forward observation team of a heavy 240mm howitzer battalion. He is responsible for drawing telephone lines from the Forward Observation Post, from where his captain directs artillery fire, to the Fire Direction Center in the rear. On June 28, he drives off the ramps of an LST (Landing Ship Troops) onto a beach in Normandy at the wheel of his weapons carrier, a pickup truck armed with a .50 machine gun and loaded with telephone equipment and wire. He vividly recalls: "We came on a small hamlet, a small cute town and they had a sign up: "Buvez Coca-Cola" (Drink Coca-Cola) I'll never forget that sign!" Before the fierce battle of St-Lo, all the men in Victor's units are served steak dinners, something they take as an bad omen: "You know how they cook you your last meal or something? We never got steak before."

When the Battle of the Bulge breaks out, Victor's battalion is supporting British forces in the Netherlands. The battalion is rushed to the St. Vith area. Repairing shot out telephone wires on the front line in combat, day or night is a crucial and perilous job. Victor recalls a particular occasion when the house his team was using as an observation post came under heavy shelling. Adding a grim and surreal touch of humor to the situation, a fellow soldier started playing the funeral march on an old accordion he had just found.

Men of the 82nd Airborne
Division near Werbormont.
U.S. Army photo.

The Soldier's Pack

A soldier carries all his personal equipment, clothing and belongings in his backpack and duffle bag (A). It is not unusual for an infantryman to be separated from his duffle bag for weeks or months at a time. Francis Gaudere of the 119th infantry division drops off his duffle bag when he lands in France shortly after D-day and would not see it again until after the war. It is up to quartermaster men to transport and store duffle bags while their owners are fighting. To help keep the bags organized, they are marked with routing numbers or color codes in paint or chalk. In October 1944, Robert Cotlowitz of the 26th Infantry "Yankee" Division is temporarily assigned to a warehouse near Nancy, France. He describes the facility as a dilapidated, rat-infested shed about as long as a football field with enormous piles of duffel bags roughly organized by company in alphabetical order.[79] Cotlowitz is tasked with retrieving the bags of the dead soldiers, so that their personal belongings, minus potentially embarrassing items, can be sent home to their next of kin. The M-1928 haversack (B) is based on a World War I concept with a trench-friendly narrow profile. The GIs view it as one of the Army's most impractical pieces of equipment. Starting in 1944, it is phased out in favor of the more sensible combat pack (C), which consists of a small combat pack on top and a larger detachable Cargo pack with a carrying handle. The musette bag (D) is a popular alternative to the combat pack. It is originally meant for airborne troops: Two straps hook up to the front of combat suspenders and hang over the belly during parachute jumps, but the straps are long enough for the bag to be swung over the head and worn as a backpack. With an optional strap, the musette bag can also be carried over a shoulder.

M1928 Haversack

The main component of the M1928 pack is the Haversack (A) with shoulder straps that attach with snap hooks to the front and back of the pistol or ammunition belt (B). The haversack opens up as a cross-shaped piece of canvas. Contents are placed over the center and the flaps are folded over and secured with straps and buckles. The Pouch, Meat Can M1928 (C), a bag designed to contain the mess kit, attaches to the cover of the haversack. The Carrier, Pack, M1928, (D) known by the soldiers as the "diaper," is a detachable extension that holds the bedroll (E). It links to the haversack with a quick-release leather strap (F) threaded though buttonholes. The entrenching tool (G) is suspended from a grommeted tab sandwiched between the haversack and the mess kit pouch. The bayonet and its scabbard (H) hangs from two grommets on the left side. Thus assembled, all these components form what was know as a soldier's pack containing almost all his equipment, including ammunition, the first aid kit (I) and canteen (J). The photo on the facing page illustrates the typical contents of a full pack. They include the toiletry kit (K), meat can (L) and silverware (M), rations (N), spare socks (O) and underwear (P), ammunition (Q) and rifle bore cleaner (R) which is sized to fit in one of the ammunition belt pockets. The bedroll (E) is formed by rolling the blanket (S), shelter half (T), tent poles, (U) and stakes (V) and sometimes extra articles of clothing tightly together. Fully loaded, a pack can exceed thirty pounds. Most soldiers lighten their load by discarding anything not absolutely necessary. The toiletry bag and meat can are among the first articles to go. The M-1928 pack is unpopular. Packing and unpacking it is tedious, and the addition of the bedroll make it impossible to sit comfortably. Because all the components are assembled by a complicated system of tabs, straps, buckles and hooks, one cannot quickly drop off the haversack without also shedding everything else, including ammunition.

These men of the 2nd Infantry Division, clearly under-equipped for the snow and cold, are taking cover in a ditch near Rocherath-Krinkelt. U.S. National Archives.

Telephones and Radios

In spite of rapid progress in electronics, portable two-way radios remain unreliable, particularly in the Ardennes where bad weather and hilly, wooded terrain severely limit their range. The SCR-536 "Handie Talkie" (A) has a useful range of a few hundred feet. The thirty-pound, backpack SCR-300 "Walkie Talkie" (see photo on opposite page) has a range of up to ten miles under good conditions. Radio capable of ranges in the tens or hundreds of miles equip vehicles, but they are too bulky and consume too much power to be useful to foot soldiers. Consequently, telephones remain the primary method of communication with radios used only as back up.

The EE-8 Phone (B) is the most compact field telephone. Contained in a canvas or leather bag, it runs on two 1.5 Volt D-cell batteries. A pair of phones can be used for point-to-point communication. Three or more can be networked via switchboards. To initiate a call, one turns a small crank (C). This generates enough current to ring the phone at the other end of the line. Alternatively, remembers John McAuliffe, a mortar man with the 87th Infantry Division: "You could pick up the phone and

whistle to get attention on the other end." Turning the crank is also a quick way to test the telephone. If it cranks too easily, it means that there is no load because of a break in the line. The twenty-pound TP-9 phone (D) features a built-in tube amplifier to achieve a longer range.

Establishing telephone lines between fluid elements and command posts in the rear is a crucial, complicated and often dangerous task. Sergeant Armand Boisseau, a lineman of the 941st Field Artillery wrote: "We were under constant threat of German snipers, land mines and booby traps. Each time we were sent out to lay or repair broken communications wire, we all had to keep a watchful eye for these personal hazards.[80]"

Veteran John McAuliffe recalls that his mortar platoon was always connected: "The headquarters was only a half mile away, and the platoon had contact with division, division had contact with regiment, you know, right down the line." Each platoon is responsible for installing new lines as they moved along: "We just cut the line, left

Above: A radio operator carrying a SCR-300 radio. Opposite page: A command team of the 90th Infantry Division is working the phone from a burned-out house in Wiltz, Luxembourg in January 1945. U.S. Signal Corps photo.

it there and wherever you went for your next position, you ran wire again. You can imagine the wire that was left all over Europe after the war!"

Front line wireman James Matthews of the 3rd Armored Division remembers that his truck carried about twenty-two, mile-long spools of wire. He and his crew moved up with the troops during the day and laid out wire at night under cover of darkness. He describes the laborious process: "The wire truck crawls at a snail's pace unreeling spools of wire. Our jeep is following the wire trail. There are two of us picking up the wire about every ten feet and tying it off the road on a tree or bush or post. It's slow going. We get about one mile of wire down and tied every two hours." Many wire crews are not as zealous. Since most lines serve no more than a few days or weeks before being abandoned, wire is often hastily laid right on the ground alongside roads. Cpl Kenneth Yockey of the 87th Infantry Division and his wire crew are billeted around Tillet when his sergeant wakes him one night because his telephone is out. Kenneth and his driver go out to inspect the line. He wrote: "It was a crisp cold bitter night. I soon found the break. Some tanks and halftracks had chewed the wires up to look like smithereens. Rather than splicing the break, we laid new lines and after checking to see that you could talk on them we then proceeded to use the "idiot stick" and sling the lines up into the trees, as we should have done in the first place.[81]"

Safe Conduct

John Cipolla of the 101st Airborne Division is in Bastogne the day before Christmas. The whining of incoming German artillery sends everyone scurrying for foxholes, but instead of the usual explosions and mayhem, leaflets come drifting down. He describes them as follows: "One had a picture of a little girl. 'Daddy, I'm so afraid.' Next to the picture was a note intended to make the men homesick: their families and sweethearts missed them; Christmas was a time to be with those people, not in a no-man's land so far away from home! 'Man, have you thought about it? What if you don't come back? What of those loved ones?' the note ended: 'Well soldier, peace on earth, goodwill toward men - for where there's a will, there's a way ... only 500 yards ahead and Merry Christmas.'"[40]

Armies on both sides wage psychological warfare with pamphlets dropped from aircraft or fired in special propaganda artillery shells. These shells are packed with tight rolls of thousands of pamphlets and a small powder charge. When subjected to the air stream at high speed, high above the ground, the pamphlets disperse over large areas. The Americans are well aware of increasing numbers of Germans who, conscious of having lost the war, are eager to give themselves up, but fear being shot as they try to surrender. Exploiting the German penchant for official procedures and paperwork, they develop a safe conduct leaflet designed with intricate guilloché patterns to look like a legal document signed by the Allied Supreme Commander Dwight Eisenhower himself. The document reads in both English and German: "The German soldier who carries this safe conduct is using it as a sign of his genuine wish to give himself up. He is to be disarmed, to be well looked after, to receive food and medical attention as required, and to be removed from the danger zone as soon as possible."

M1 Helmet

The M1 is a two-piece helmet consisting of a lightweight liner fitted inside a manganese steel shell. The liner is made of compressed cardboard impregnated with phenolic resin. The steel shell is coated with matte paint with inclusions of ground cork. It is discovered that despite this textured finish, the helmet becomes conspicuously shiny when wet or greasy. This problem is mitigated with the use of camouflage netting. In addition to the protection it provides, the detachable steel shell proves useful in a multitude of ways: It is used as a seat, bucket, washbasin and occasionally as a cooking pot or scoop for digging. Veteran Joe Landry, a truck driver for the 776th Anti-Aircraft Artillery Battalion remembers: "We used to clean up a helmet nice and shiny and we hung it in the exhaust. Let the truck run for ten minutes and heat up the water to make coffee or shave or whatever you want. And sometimes you'd use that helmet for other reasons, especially the guys riding the back of the truck. Every once in a while if there is a truck in front of you, you'd see a guy empty the helmet out the tailgate." Because many soldiers live outdoors for weeks at a time, they joke that they carry their homes on their heads. Some decorate the inside with photos of loved ones or pinup girls. Veteran Gordon Hatch of the 6th Armored Division remembers that he wore his helmet day and night, even while sleeping, removing it only for shaving.

Bill Gast, 743ʳᵈ Tank Battalion and his Wife Betty Remember

Left: Betty Ludwig and Bill Gast during a brief furlough in June 1943.
Right: Bill kept photos of his girlfriend Betty under a see-through grip of his M1911 pistol. The grips had been fashioned by a Belgian civilian from Plexiglas recovered from a downed German airplane.

a new role as Liaison Corporal, operating radio equipment from a jeep. On one of his reconnaissance missions, Bill is accompanied by a very apprehensive Army cook serving as a jeep driver. The two men are sent out ahead of their unit to select a building as new headquarters. After Bill has selected a suitable house, he spots a German soldier at the edge of nearby woods. The situation is extremely tense as Bill and his driver are armed only with a Thompson sub-machine gun and a pistol and they suspect that the German is not alone. Soon, the German approaches the jeep with his hands on his helmet, followed by 119 of his comrades. When the 743ʳᵈ takes possession of its new headquarters, it is greeted by Bill, the cook driver and 120 prisoners of war.

Bill Gast is born in Lancaster, Pennsylvania on September 4, 1924. When he reaches the draft age of 18, he volunteers for service and is sent to Armor School in Fort Knox, Kentucky to be trained as a tank driver and mechanic. In preparation for the North African campaign, Bill is sent to Camp Laguna in the Arizona desert. "It was so hot," remembers Bill "that you could take a shower with your clothes on and you were dry by the time you walked back to your tent." The fighting in North Africa comes to an end before Bill's training is completed, so his unit is directed to England to prepare for D-day. Bill and his crew repeatedly rehearse landing their Sherman tank on British beaches. "We never really knew if it was an exercise or the real thing." recalls Bill. On June 6, 1944, he drives his tank onto Omaha Beach ten minutes ahead of H-Hour. "Bullets are hitting the tank like throwing marbles at a car." remembers Bill. His view of the beach through a narrow periscope slit is restricted by smoke and sand kicked up by bullets and explosions. To this day, Bill is haunted by the thought that he may have driven his tank over the bodies of the dead and wounded soldiers lying all around. The tank commander sitting in the turret directs Bill by kicking him in the left or right shoulder until they reach the precarious safety of a seawall.

Over the following weeks, Bill's unit is involved in intense fighting in Normandy's hedgerows. During the battle of Mortain, Bill's crew loses three commanders. He serves as commander himself until he is wounded by shrapnel on August 10, 1944.

The war has separated Bill from his high-school sweetheart Betty Ludwig. She remembers being one of countless "war widows" who wrote letters every night to their special soldiers overseas. Consumed by heartache and worry, Betty eventually becomes frustrated by Bill's sporadic mail. She remembers her mom pleading: "Bill might be sick or wounded in the hospital unable to write." And her dad teasing: "He's too busy with all those French girls!" She finally writes to Bill: "From now on, I will only answer your letters. I am tired of this one-way correspondence." The next day, remembers Betty: "We were notified that Bill had been wounded in Mortain, France and was recovering in a field hospital. I immediately wrote and promised to keep writing, no matter what!"

Bill is never officially discharged from the hospital where he underwent surgery. The hospital is bombed and in the turmoil that ensues, he simply walks off in search of his unit. By the time he catches up with the 743ʳᵈ in Belgium, his position as a tank driver had been filled. Bill takes on

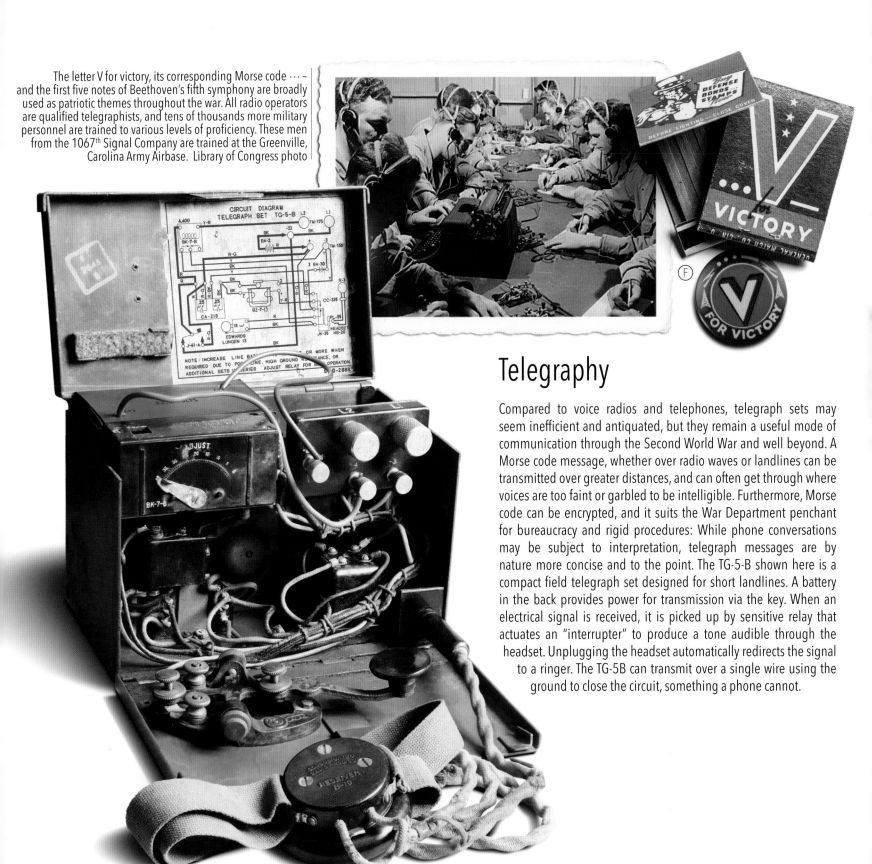

The letter V for victory, its corresponding Morse code ···– and the first five notes of Beethoven's fifth symphony are broadly used as patriotic themes throughout the war. All radio operators are qualified telegraphists, and tens of thousands more military personnel are trained to various levels of proficiency. These men from the 1067th Signal Company are trained at the Greenville, Carolina Army Airbase. Library of Congress photo

Telegraphy

Compared to voice radios and telephones, telegraph sets may seem inefficient and antiquated, but they remain a useful mode of communication through the Second World War and well beyond. A Morse code message, whether over radio waves or landlines can be transmitted over greater distances, and can often get through where voices are too faint or garbled to be intelligible. Furthermore, Morse code can be encrypted, and it suits the War Department penchant for bureaucracy and rigid procedures: While phone conversations may be subject to interpretation, telegraph messages are by nature more concise and to the point. The TG-5-B shown here is a compact field telegraph set designed for short landlines. A battery in the back provides power for transmission via the key. When an electrical signal is received, it is picked up by sensitive relay that actuates an "interrupter" to produce a tone audible through the headset. Unplugging the headset automatically redirects the signal to a ringer. The TG-5B can transmit over a single wire using the ground to close the circuit, something a phone cannot.

155 mm M1 "Long Tom" Gun

The 155 mm gun nicknamed "Long Tom" is introduced just prior to World War II. It fires 95-pound shells up to 15 miles. Cannoneers select from a variety of shells including High Explosive (A), smoke, white phosphorous and even propaganda shells loaded with pamphlets (See page 97). Before firing, the lifting ring at the nose of the shell is removed and replaced with a fuse set to detonate either upon impact, after a set time, or by proximity (See page 103). The shell is loaded and rammed through the breech. The propellant charge comes separately in a protective canister (B). It consists of seven bags of gunpowder bundled together; one or more bags are usually removed from the bundle, since maximum range is seldom needed. The bundle is placed behind the shell, the breech is closed, armed with a primer and the gun is ready to fire.

Field artillery battalions typically include three artillery batteries of four guns each, and a headquarters battery that includes the Fire Direction Center (FDC). The FDC receives and prioritizes fire support requests as map coordinates. By plotting the target coordinates on their own map, and by comparing it to the known location of the gun batteries with rulers and protractors, the FDC can work out the distance and direction of the target and thus the corresponding azimuth and elevation of the guns. To compensate for such factors as temperature, humidity, wind, altitude difference and even barrel wear, the FDC refers to books containing thousands of pre-calculated tables. Even so, observers on the ground or in light aircraft are often needed to home in on the target.

These men are posing in front of their gun, which they have whitewashed to make it less conspicuous in the snow. U.S. National Archives.

Overcoats, Coats and Jackets

The Melton overcoat (A) is named after a type of heavy wool cloth that originated in Melton, England. This standard-issue, double-breasted overcoat is deemed unsuitable for combat because it is too heavy and stiff. It is ordinarily worn as part of the dress uniform or on non-combat duties. It is nonetheless used by front-line troops during the Battle of the Bulge for lack of more practical cold-weather clothing. The overcoat is warm but can become very heavy when wet or encrusted with snow. Staff Sergeant James Cullen of the 3rd Armored Division wrote: "The overcoats quickly acquired a coating of ice and snow from the knees down as we plowed through the deep snow. That made climbing onto a tank next to impossible and walking extremely difficult.[82]" In a hard frost, the problem is compounded by sweat evaporating from the body then freezing as it nears the outer surface of the overcoat. Over time, it turns into a sort of frozen carapace to the point where the exhausted men can no longer bear to wear them. Private first class Donald Schoo of the 80th Infantry Division recalls a man who became stuck in his halftrack: "His overcoat was wet when he got in and it froze so he couldn't get out.[62]"

The Mackinaw Jacket (B) is named after the great lakes region where it originated in the 19th century. The traditional Mackinaw coat was made of heavy plaid wool blankets and was popular with loggers and outdoorsmen. The Army version features a windproof, water-repellent cotton shell over a blanket wool liner. Some soldiers are reluctant to wear "macks" for fear that they might be mistaken for officers by German snipers.

The combat jacket (C) is better known as a "tanker's jacket" because it was originally designed for tank crews. The zipper, and knitted collar, waistband and cuffs are less likely to get caught in the cramped space of an armored vehicle. These same features also make it particularly effective at blocking out the cold. The tanker's jacket is very popular but it is only issued in limited quantities hence it is mostly worn by officers.

Soldiers of the band of the 28th Division in Wiltz, Luxembourg on December 20, 1944. U.S. National Archives photo..

The New Shell with the Funny Fuse

The proximity fuse, also known as the pozit fuse, features a miniature radar that detonates a shell when it detects the proximity of any large object, including the ground. It is of such strategic importance that before the Battle of the Bulge, it has never been deployed against land forces for fear that it might be captured and reverse-engineered or jammed.

The pozit fuse is the brainchild of British scientists. Its development and production in the United States are surrounded with as much secrecy as the atomic bomb. Although the fuse is ingeniously simple in theory, building it presents enormous technical challenges. At the time, electronic devices are constructed of bulky and fragile glass vacuum tubes. Each component has to be miniaturized and re-engineered to withstand the fantastic accelerations of artillery shells while retaining high levels of precision and reliability.

The pozit fuse is initially intended for anti-aircraft gunnery. A shell fitted with a proximity fuse only has to pass anywhere within 75 feet of an aerial target. Effectively, it magnifies airplanes to the size of blimps. It proves effective in the defense of the Pacific Fleet against Kamikazes and in Great Britain against V1 flying bombs. During the Battle of the Bulge, the proximity fuse is used to create air burst. An air burst is a shell that explodes above the ground rather that after hitting it. It generates a more powerful concussion and sprays shrapnel downward over a wide area. To achieve air burst with time fuses requires complex calculations, and trial and error. By the time the gunner gets the timing of his fuses right, the enemy has time to hunker down or move. The pozit fuse on the other hand, generates air burst with immediate and near total reliability, catching ground forces completely by surprise in the open.

In a letter to General Campbell, General Patton wrote: "The new shell with the funny fuse is devastating. . . I think that when all armies get this, we will have to devise some new method of warfare. . . I am glad that you all thought of it first".

The John Hopkins University Applied Physics Laboratory, founded in 1942 as part of an effort to mobilize scientists in support of the war effort, is instrumental in the development of the proximity fuse. The fuse shown here was presented by the laboratory after the war in recognition for contribution to its development. Inscriptions read: "Officials of the War and Navy Departments rate this fuse, along with radar and the atomic bomb, as one of the three outstanding scientific contributions to World War II"

M20 Armored Utility Car

The M20 armored utility car is a variant of the M8 Greyhound (pictured below). It is originally designed as a tank destroyer with a turret and a 37 mm gun, but soon proves ineffective against heavily armored German tanks. The vehicle is then re-purposed as a command and reconnaissance vehicle.

Despite its very rugged appearance, the vehicle is very lightly armored. The 7/8" steel front and 3/8" sides are only effective against small arms and shrapnel, and the 1/8" floor leaves the crew vulnerable to land mines.

Weak off-road capabilities limit the Greyhound's usefulness as a scouting vehicle. It has a tendency to bog down in mud or snow, and because of a wide turning radius, it is difficult to maneuver through wooded terrain. Nonetheless, the Greyhound fulfills important duties as a command, escort and communication vehicle. Equipped with long-range radios, it often provides an important link between the front lines and commanding officers in the rear. Over paved roads, it can achieve an impressive 55 mph. This high speed provides a measure of protection against German artillery that cannot traverse quickly enough to keep up.

The M20 accommodates up to six men. A driver and a radio operator sit in front and up to four people can sit on lateral benches in the back. The main armament consists of a .50 anti-aircraft heavy machine gun. The crew is generally equipped with carbines, grenades, bazookas and land mines stored in large exterior compartments.

Sergeant Rodney Himes and Private Alfred Gernhardt of the 84th Division shake hands with Sergeant
Angel Casey of the 11th Armored Division on January 16, 1945. U.S. National Archives.

Axis Sally

GIs across Europe are treated to regular German propaganda radio broadcasts featuring the sultry voice of an American female announcer. She refers to herself as Midge-at-the-mike, but she is better known as "Axis Sally", or sometimes "the Berlin bitch". Her programs include the most recent American music hits interspersed with scripted monologues. Flirty teasing alternates with predictions of doom and depictions of blissful domestic life: "I'm afraid you're yearning plenty for someone else, but I wonder if she isn't running around with the 4-Fs (See page 18) way back home.[3]" For maximum effect, Axis Sally sometimes includes uncanny details of Allied troop movements and goes so far as to call out specific units or even soldiers by name. During the night of December 17, as they are rushed into the Ardennes, men of the 30th Infantry Division listen to Axis Sally on their vehicle radios: "The 30th Infantry Division, the elite Roosevelt's SS troops and butchers, are en route from Aachen to Spa and Malmedy, Belgium, to try to save the 1st Army Headquarters, which is trying to retreat from the area before they are captured by our nice young German boys. You guys of the 30th Division might as well give up now, unless you want to join your comrades in a P.O.W. camp. We have already captured most of the 106th Division, and have already taken St. Vith and Malmedy, and the next will be Liège.[84]" 1st Lt Frank Towers wrote: "We were stunned, as only then did we have any clue as to where we were going, or the reason for this sudden movement.[84]"

As the German state radio broadcasts worldwide, Axis Sally often addresses American civilians and women in particular: "As one American to another, do you love the British? Well, of course the answer is no. Do the British love us? I should say not! We are fighting for them? We are shedding our good young blood for this kike war, for this British war? Oh, girl why don't you wake up!" In another broadcast she rants: "Damn Roosevelt! Damn Churchill! Damn all the Jews who made this war possible! I love America, but I do not love Roosevelt and all his kike boyfriends![85]"

Behind Axis Sally's voice is a forty-year-old American woman by the name of Mildred Gillars. Born in Maine, she studied drama as a young woman but failed to establish herself as an actress. She traveled to North Africa and Europe doing odd jobs and eventually settled in Germany where she worked as an English teacher and finally as an English-speaking announcer for the state radio. After the war, she is arrested, flown back to the United States and convicted of treason. Upon her release from prison in 1961, Gillars works as an elementary school teacher at St. Joseph Academy in Columbus, Ohio.

Her motivation for partaking in German propaganda would remain a mystery as she would carefully dodge the subject for the rest of her life.

Right: Mildred Gillars in 1948 awaiting her trial for treason. Above: Identity photos taken by the Department of Justice.

Left Behind

Bill Campbell of the 28th Infantry Division suffers from frostbitten feet during the Battle of the Bulge, but the extent of his injuries would not reveal itself until much later after he has been redeployed to the Vosges mountains in France to help clean up an area of German resistance known as the Colmar Pocket. As he marches through the city of Turckheim on February 1, 1945, Bill becomes so sick that he can no longer walk and he starts vomiting. He remembers an indignant officer inquiring: "Is this man drunk?" Aid men take him to a nearby civilian hospital. Bill recounts: "I just laid on a bed with my overcoat, my helmet and my boots still on, just fell onto the bed. Corporal Reese said: 'I'll be back.' That's the last I ever saw him." Bill wakes up three days later with his feet bandaged in a room that he shares with two German soldiers: an older infantryman and a young pilot. Although Bill cannot communicate with them, he gets along with his two roommates. One morning, about two weeks into his recovery, Bill is awoken by a commotion: "So I hobbled out of bed and went to the window. They had this guy stripped down with a Nazi flag like a skirt and they were beating the shit out of him. He was the Burgomaster of the town and he had collaborated with the Germans. He ended up in a bed next to mine."

One of the nurses speaks a little English, she comes by once in a while to chat with Bill and to keep him company. As the only American in town, and even though he is confined to the hospital, Bill becomes something of a local celebrity. He entrusts a letter to a local man who speaks English with the instruction to hand it to any American vehicle passing by. The letter explains Bill's predicament. "Being nineteen years old, I complained that I didn't have any candy, I didn't have any magazines, everything is in a foreign language". recalls Bill.

About a week later two American officers come by carrying magazines, boxes of candy and cartons of cigarettes. Bill would face more time in military hospitals and several interrogations by Army investigators who suspect that Bill might be an impostor or a deserter. He eventually finds out that his mother has received two missing in action telegraphs before receiving a third one indicating that he was safe. Bill explains: "I think that when it all boiled down, to save face, they put me down as a prisoner of war, which I didn't know until I got a letter from a POW association long after the war".

Service Shoes and Combat Boots

The U.S. Army is the first army in the world to adopt rubber-soled combat shoes. These are lighter, more durable and quieter than leather-soled hobnailed boots such as the ones worn by German soldiers. Civilians cowering in their houses can usually tell whether the soldiers passing by are American or German by the sound of their boots. At the onset of the war, ankle-high service shoes (A) are worn with heavy canvas leggings (B). These leggings are unpopular because putting them on and taking them off is tedious, the cotton laces frequently break, they soak up moisture and the strap below the sole gets caught in underbrush. In 1943, the Army introduces the first modern combat boot (C) featuring a leather cuff with two buckles that render the leggings unnecessary. James Kullen of the 3rd Armored Division remembers that as late as January 1944, his regiment was still wearing the old ankle-high boots with leggings: "We didn't learn about shoe pacs and combat boots until much later.[86]"

For durability, the combat boots are constructed with the flesh side of the leather facing out because it is less likely to crack when exposed to the elements and in theory, it absorbs shoe grease better. But these suede-like boots leave many soldiers perplexed. Herb Adams of the 82nd Airborne Division recalls: "These damned things had the leather inside out. You didn't have to walk into a puddle, you just walked by it and it sucked it up." Soldiers are supplied with cans of dubbing (D), a mixture of wood resin, neats foot oil, wax and solvents that help preserve the leather and repel water. Impregnite (E) is a similar compound designed to protect against chemical agents.

Men of the 101st Airborne Division look for their shoe size in a pile of overshoes in Bastogne on January 10, 1945. U.S. Army photo.

M3 Halftrack

Following World War I, the U.S. Army identifies the need for an lightly armored all-terrain troop carrier to improve the mobility of its infantry. Traditional trucks handle poorly off-road, particularly with the extra weight of armor plating. They bog down in mud or snow and lose traction. Fully tracked vehicles handle better, but they are slow, expensive and maintenance-heavy. The solution is a compromise based on the work of French engineer Adolph Kégresse. The M3 Halftrack is based on a conventional truck chassis fitted with rubber-encased tracks on the rear axle. Built much like a regular truck, the M3 halftrack developed by the White Motor Company is economical and its operation and maintenance require little extra training. Configured as a personnel carrier, the M3 is large enough for a thirteen-men platoon with all its equipment, but in combat, the 1/4" steel armor proves insufficient. It provides no overhead protection and it is breached by armor-piercing machine gun rounds, which then ricochet inside to devastating effect.

The M3 is also used as a platform for various weapons. The famous M16 Multiple Gun Motor Carriage version shown below is an anti-aircraft configuration that features an M45 quad-mount turret with four .50 caliber M2 Browning heavy machine guns. During the Battle of the Bulge, it is very successfully put to work against ground forces, earning the grimly evocative nicknames of "krautmower" and "meat-chopper."

Overshoes and Shoepacs

Since leather combat boots cannot be made impermeable no matter how much grease and wax is applied, the army distributes rubber overshoes that fit over the combat boots. The overshoes are invaluable against the cold, but they are clunky, noisy and they wear out quickly. Staff Sergeant Henry Mooseker wrote: "Your feet seemed four times as heavy. This was a clumsy arrangement but they helped keep our feet warm and dry but they came after the worst weather was over.[67]" Bill Campbell of the 28th Infantry Division recalls: "The soles got so smooth. I was walking on this road, and I started sliding off the hill. So I tried to get traction and I finally got hold of a little tree to stop myself. One of the things they drill into you is they always shoot at stragglers, and here I am, two hundred yards behind my troop and I'm struggling to get my feet moving. I finally got down to my hands

and knees and crawled to a safe spot and then I caught up."

Some enterprising soldiers stuff their overshoes with hay, or improvise liners with wool blankets to convert them into snow boots. Bill Gast of the 743rd Tank Battalion recalls that he found a sheep skin in a barn and gave it to his friend and jeep driver Norman Hamilton: "He took that sheep skin and made a pair of booties for himself and for me that fit inside our four-buckle galoshes. I mean, you couldn't have gone anywhere and bought anything like that! So we just had toasty warm feet."

Shoepacs consist of a rubber shoe with a laced waterproof leather top. The shoepacks are roomy enough for heavy felt insoles and one or two pairs of heavy wool socks. Thus worn, they are effective in cold, wet conditions, but only if the socks and insole can be dried regularly to prevent perspiration from building up. Unfortunately, shoepacs are in short supplies. Most units would not see them until late January.

The M1A1 with a folding stock is the airborne version of the M1 carbine (See page 54).

The Siege of Bastogne

The southern prong of the German attack quickly sweeps through Luxembourg, overwhelming the 28th Infantry Division. The momentum of the German spearhead points to the city of Bastogne as an obligatory waypoint. Bastogne is the region's largest town and a nexus of major roads. Eisenhower designates it as the fallback position to regroup and make a stand. On December 17, he commits the 98th and 101st Airborne Divisions held in reserve in Mourmelon-le-Grand, France. The Airborne troops have only a few hours to prepare before they are rushed to the Ardennes. Poorly equipped against the cold, they are packed so tightly in open trucks that they cannot sit down. Although originally destined to Werbomont, the men of the 101st under Brigadier General McAuliffe are redirected towards Bastogne. Along the way, they witness hordes of defeated men from the 28th, glad to surrender whatever ammunition they have left. On December 19, during a conference with his senior commanders in Verdun, France, Eisenhower asks Patton, whose third army is located south of the Bulge, how long it would take to launch a counter offensive. Patton boasts that he can attack within 48 hours.

Men and tanks of the 10th Armored Division have already reached Bastogne. Organized into task forces named after their commanders, team Desobry, team Booth, team O'Hara and team Cherry hurriedly establish roadblocks east of Bastogne. Team Desobry is hit particularly hard in Noville, but reinforced by elements of the 101st Airborne and the 705th Tank Destroyer Battalion, it gives the Germans the impression of a much larger presence before falling back on Bastogne. Had the Germans persisted in a frontal attack, they would likely have

overrun the Americans, but they hesitate and decide to circumvent Bastogne to attack from the south and west. This delay allows the 101st to organize a defensive perimeter while additional reinforcements continue to arrive. Stragglers from the 28th Infantry Division and various other units retreating through Bastogne are aggregated into a reserve force designated team Snafu. By December 21, the Americans defenders are surrounded and outnumbered five to one. But having fallen behind his timetable, General von Lüttwitz sends the bulk of his panzers on towards Marche-en-Famenne, leaving only a small armored detachment along with General Kokott's 26th Volksgrenadiers to reduce Bastogne. Prospects are grim for McAuliffe. His men are deficient in

Lieutenant General Danahy, Brigadier General McAuliffe and Lieutenant Colonel Kinnard of the 101st Airborne Division after the battle of Bastogne.

Above: Soldiers from the 101st Airborne Division "Screaming Eagles" attend Christmas Mass in Bastogne with their rifles at the ready. Right: The Heintz barracks serve as the headquarters of Brigadier General McAuliffe. A small group of C-47 cargo planes are dropping supplies in the background. U.S. Army photo.

winter clothing, ammunition and food. With no possibility of evacuation, the casualties count grows quickly. Snow and low cloud cover make air support and resupply impossible. On December 22, four German soldiers are observed waving a white flag as they approach. One of them explains in English that they are delivering an ultimatum. The letter addressed to the "U.S.A. Commander" points out the fact that Bastogne is surrounded and gives the Americans two hours to surrender or else face annihilation by Artillery.

A sleep-deprived McAuliffe is awoken from a nap. Lieutenant Colonel Harry Kinnard of the 101st Airborne Division recalls: "General McAuliffe mistakenly thought that these were Germans who wanted to surrender to us, but we disabused him of that thought very quickly and we said: 'No, they want us to surrender.' Tony McAuliffe then said: 'Us, surrender? Aw, nuts!' Then he went on and he said: 'Well, I wonder if we ought to answer them.' And we all felt that it required an answer. I spoke up and said: 'What you first said would be hard to beat.' And Tony said: 'What do you mean?' And I said: 'You said nuts!'[4]"

Word of McAuliffe's one-word response spreads rapidly and boosts the morale of the American defenders. Captain Jack Prior, a doctor in the 10th Armored Division wrote: "The news that we were surrounded also had a curious effect upon our men – such remarks were heard as: 'they've got us surrounded, the poor bastards,' or 'surrounded, good – now we can attack on all sides.'[11]" The Germans do not have enough artillery shells to carry out their threat. They nonetheless bombard the town and launch a series of probing attacks.

On December 23, the sky finally clears. Dr. Prior wrote: "Hundreds of C-47s droned over Bastogne and multicolored parachutes fell to earth – each color representing a category of supplies. Food, ammunition, blankets, medical items were eagerly gathered.[11]" The parachute drops are repeated the following day.

Hugh Roush of the 101st Airborne Division Wrote: "As we retrieved the bundles, first we cut up the bag material and wrapped our feet in it, to help keep our feet warm – then we proceeded to take care of the supplies and the ammunition we so sorely needed. How great it was to have warm feet! Of course, along with the clear weather, we now had air support – P51s, P47s, P38s. Things surely were looking up! We felt we could endure most anything now.[88]"

On Christmas Eve, Patton sends the following message to McAuliffe: "Xmas eve present coming up. Hold on.[89]" But the advance of Patton's 4th Armored Division is frustrated by stiff German opposition. That evening, Luftwaffe planes drop flares over Bastogne followed by bombs that destroy a makeshift aid station and kill 21 people, including a young Belgian nurse by the name of Renée Lemaire (See page 113). On Christmas Day, the Germans launch their last major assault in the form of successive attacks from the west. Some panzers penetrate the town but the defenders manage to shift their forces and repulse one attack after the other.

Just before 5:00 PM on December 26, the leading tank of Patton's 4th Armored Division reaches Bastogne from the direction of Assenois. The siege of Bastogne has been lifted.

Other events on the Elsenborn Ridge, St Vith and La Gleize prove more dramatic and more consequential than the siege of Bastogne, yet they never achieve the same notoriety. Bastogne is covered abundantly in the press, in part because news correspondents are much more present in the area. Christmas under siege, the colorful response of General McAuliffe, the supply airdrops, and General Patton's charge, capture the imagination and eclipse other battles. The "Battered Bastards of the Bastion of Bastogne" seem to redeem the panic and routs of previous days and become the symbol of American fortitude.

Frostbite and Trench Foot

As he looks at a period poster suggesting "Keep your feet dry and clean" Bill Campbell of the 112th Infantry Regiment laughs: "Now how the hell do you do that? We were always moving. Supplies were non-existent." Leather combat boots cannot be made impermeable, no matter how much dubbing and shoe polish is applied. In the mud, rain and snow of the Ardennes, socks soon become wet and lose any insulation value. Galoshes and winter clothing are in short supplies and as Francis Gaudere of the 119th Infantry Division bitterly recalls: "Before all that stuff came up, the rear echelon were all equipped with the stuff that we should have had." Famous wartime cartoonist Bill Mauldin captures with humor the importance of dry socks in one of his Willie and Joe cartoons: The two despondent soldiers are sitting down with their feet in water and mud. Willie leans over to Joe and says: "Yestiddy ya saved my life and I swore I'd pay ya back. Here's my last pair of dry socks.[38]"

Soldiers are encouraged to keep at least two pairs of socks at all time. While they are wearing one, the other is carried under the helmet liner or stuffed under one's shirt where body heat will eventually dry it. Sometimes new socks are handed out along with food rations or mail. Soldiers are also instructed to rub their feet daily, to use foot powder and allow their shoes to dry every night. Obviously, this often proves impossible. Herb Adams of the 98th Parachute Infantry Division explains: "All I had was two pairs of socks, very thin socks. Of course during the battle, there was no way that you could take off your shoes. Your feet would swell to the point where you could not put your shoes back on. […] What's the hell, there may not be any tomorrow, so why do I have to go to the hospital for my feet, it's too late now. Once they start freezing to a certain point, there is no more feeling whatsoever. The pain is gone, so now they are just stubs down there for you to walk on."

During the Battle of the Bulge, more than 15,000 men are evacuated for frostbite or trench foot due to inadequate clothing or footwear. Superficial frostbite causes blisters that sometimes turn black. Deep-tissue frostbite usually results in the necrosis of extremities such as ears, noses, fingers or toes. Trench foot occurs when wet shoes are worn for extended periods, particularly in cold but not necessarily freezing conditions. The resulting lesions are nearly identical to frostbites. Frostbite and trench foot are slow to heal and often lead to gangrene and infections. They typically cause the sufferers to be bedridden or wheelchair-bound for weeks or months and often result in amputations. Herb Adams who arrived in the Ardennes on December 18 would not get the opportunity to care for his feet until February 5 when he is evacuated due to a shrapnel wound to the thigh. When medics take off his boots at the aid station, his feet are black and the skin is peeling off. About a week later in a hospital in Paris, Herb is told that gangrene has set in and that both his feet would be amputated the following morning. Fortunately the operation is postponed and Herb is evacuated to yet another hospital where he shares a room with about fifteen other frostbitten patients, all bedridden with their

Medics are charged with inspecting the feet of the soldiers on a regular basis to detect and treat early signs of frostbites or trench foot. U.S. Army photo.

feet elevated. Herb recalls the visit of another doctor who struck him as very young. Having served in the Aleutian Islands of Alaska, the young doctor had treated numerous cases of frostbite: "He took a hold of my big toe and he wiggled it and said: 'What does that tell you? If the big toe doesn't come off, I can save them. Get your feet off of that, get them down. You guys are gonna go for a walk.'" Herb recalls the doctor's precise instruction to an MP as some of the patients express their reluctance: "The first guy who says he's not gonna walk, you stick your bayonet up his ass and that's an order!" Herb describes his gruesome and painful recovery as follows: "When you are walking, your legs start swelling and swelling. After a while you'd stop, a medic would examine you, and if you couldn't take anymore, he'd put you in the ambulance. By the time I got back, my legs were like balloons. And as the guy wanted to check my leg, one of my feet burst open. He was covered from one end to the other. And the stink! It was like some animal that had been dead for a week! After that, they'd take a five gallon bucket and put my feet in there, they'd lance your foot, or leg somewhere down there, and you wouldn't begin to believe the gunk and stuff that would pour out. Each day, you'd do it, it becomes less. As far as I know, everyone of the guys that went in with me came out with their feet."

Norval Williams of the 80th Infantry Division is sent to the rear for dental work. When he asks a medic for a new pair of socks, the medic notices that his feet have been frozen. Williams wrote: "The beds in the trench foot ward were made up by turning up the top sheet and blanket at the bottom of the bed allowing your feet to remain uncovered which helped to increase the circulation to the feet. And, if while sleeping you may accidentally draw your feet up beneath the covers, the nurse would come by and drag your feet back out. The frozen feet turned black by the skin cells dying and new skin cells had to grow back to replace the dead cells, along with therapy such as whirlpool baths and picking up marbles with your toes to increase circulation.[90]"

Francis Gaudere of the 119th Infantry Division is representative of many veterans who came home with both hands and both feet but never fully recovered from their many brushes with hypothermia: "My feet practically froze and my hands… They are still affected. My feet are never warm. My hands are always cold. At home, all the time I put my hands like this (Under his armpits) to keep them warm"

The Angels of Bastogne

In December of 1944 Augusta Chiwy and Renée Lemaire, two young Belgian registered nurses have returned home to Bastogne for the holidays. When they arrive, the town is safely under American control, but they soon find themselves in the thick of the German offensive. Captain Jack Prior's aid station is severely understaffed, low on supplies, and without electricity or running water. He wrote after the war: "I was holding over one hundred patients, of whom about thirty were very seriously injured litter patients. The patients who had head, chest and abdominal wounds could only face certain slow death since there was no chance of surgical procedures – we had no surgical talent among us and there was not so much as a can of ether or a scalpel to be had in the city.[11]" On December 21, Augusta and Renée approach Dr. Prior to volunteer their help. Reflecting the racial bias of the time, Dr. Prior would later praise the efforts of Renée by name while referring to Augusta, who is born to a black Congolese mother, only as "the Congo girl". He wrote: "They played different roles among the dying – Renée shrank away from the fresh, gory trauma, while the Congo girl was always in the thick of the splinting, dressing, and hemorrhage control. Renée preferred to circulate among the litter patients, sponging, feeding them, and distributing the few medications we had (sulfa pills and plasma). The presence of these two girls was a morale factor of the highest order.[11]" On December 23, when the sky clears over Bastogne, planes drop desperately needed supplies. On several occasions, Renée runs to the backyard in the hope of picking up a white parachute with which she plans to make her wedding dress, but she always comes back empty-handed. The following day, the makeshift hospital is hit by two aerial bombs. Renée is among thirty people who die in the burning rubble. Augusta survives the blast and continues her work, going so far as wearing an American uniform to pick up the wounded on the battlefield. Dr. Prior would later wrap Renée's remains in a white silk parachute before returning them to her parents. Much has been written about Renée Lemaire, the angel of Bastogne, but Augusta is mostly forgotten. In 2011, thanks to the work of British historian Martin King, her courage and devotion were finally recognized. She received the Belgian Order of the Crown Medal, and the American Civilian Award for Humanitarian Service. She died in 2015 at the age of 94.

Looting and Vandalism

American soldiers are generally respectful of civilians and even show great generosity towards them. Nonetheless, instances of looting and vandalism are frequent. For a small minority of soldiers inclined to thievery, an evacuated and bomb-ravaged town is too strong a temptation to resist. Even soldiers who would never steal or trespass in civilian life, think little of rummaging through homes and "liberating" any food, drinks, valuables or souvenirs they want. Evacuees returning to houses that have been occupied by Americans in their absence often find that the place has been ransacked. In some cases, furniture has been thrown out of windows to clear space or burned as firewood. Muddy footprints are everywhere and provisions, blankets and valuables are missing.

Many soldiers feel that the hardship they are enduring entitles them to some looting. In a world dominated by violence, destruction and death, moral and judicial boundaries are blurred and survival or immediate gratification trump scruples.

Herb Adams of the 82nd Airborne Division regrets the behavior of his squad entering the house of an elderly woman and her grandson in Remouchamps: "We were so relieved to get some heat and what have you. I had some friends and the first thing they did is run into the bedroom and jump into the bed. We were running around the house like a bunch of rats, hollering and screaming for joy." Herb's sergeant remedies the situation the following day, but not before the old lady and young boy have been forced to spend the night on a floor.

This photo of the bomb-ravaged streets of Bastogne illustrates the blurred line between found and stolen goods. U.S. Army photo.

In a report to Belgian Prime Minister Hubert Pierlot, the Mayor of Bastogne, Léon Jacquemin complains: "While it pains me to accuse an allied army of something as reprehensible as looting, we must protest that the town has been the object of shameless plunder. A large number of soldiers have looted and ransacked public buildings as well as private homes. If laundry, blankets and stoves were indispensable to soldiers cut off from their lines, it is completely unacceptable for radios to be taken and sold or exchanged 50 km away, for vaults to be cut open with acetylene torches, for drawers and cupboards to be emptied on the floor and trampled.[91]" Jacquemin also complained that watches had been stolen from a store window and stripped of their works, the soldier keeping only the gold cases.[92] He points out that Major General Maxwell Taylor of the 101st and Lieutenant Sherman Hoyt, the head of a Civil Affair detachment did all they could to stop the looting, but that the effort was hindered by some among the Military Police that were themselves guilty of looting.

The Army PX

Among the more popular spots on any military base is the Post Exchange, or PX for short. The PX is a convenience store where soldiers can purchase cigarettes, snacks, toiletries, stationery, magazines, and other such sundries. The PX is usually staffed by civilians under military governance and given latitude to adapt the merchandise to local needs and wants. All of its profit are used to finance recreation opportunities for the soldier. PXs in larger military camps are as well stocked as department stores. Many PXs also feature snack bars with soft drinks, sandwiches, ice cream, and what is known as 3.2 beer: Beer with a maximum alcohol content of 3.2% - about half that of ordinary beer.

PX stores accompany the soldiers overseas and are opened in camps or cities were large numbers of American soldiers are present. Some mobile PXs operate out of trucks or tents. In addition to filling day-to-day needs, PXs are important morale boosters. Battle-weary soldiers on foreign soil find comfort in familiar American brands and even small convenience items take on an aura of luxury. Soldiers can arrange to send home gifts they select from the PX's *Gift Catalog for Every Occasion*. Unfortunately, PXs are not immune to the supply shortages that beset the Army. PX stocks are given low priority on the strained supply convoys, and they are prime targets for black marketeers. Soldiers complain that basic commodities such as toothpaste and shaving cream are often in very short supply and that they have to rely on packages from home.

A PX for the 1st Infantry Division in Spa, Belgium. U.S. National Archives.

Fallen from the Sky

On August 17, 1943, ten-year-old Marcel Schmetz witnesses a seemingly endless procession of American B-17 "Flying Fortresses" high above his parents' farm in Clermont, Belgium. They are on their way to one of the most ambitious strategic bombing missions of the war. Three hundred and sixty-seven bombers with support from hundreds of fighters attempt to cripple Germany's aircraft factories in the Schweinfurt-Regensburg area. The size of the bomber force is so astonishing that Marcel's school is dismissed, leaving him and his comrades to gaze at the extraordinary sight. German fighters are dispatched to confront the bombers. Marcel observes two of them attacking one of the bombers. There is an explosion and the bomber falls to earth. Marcel and his dad hop on their bicycles and head for the crash site, but by the time they arrive near the burning plane wreck, German soldiers have already cordoned off the area. The bombers achieve limited success and sixty of them are lost along with their ten-men crews. Marcel would find out later that the plane that has been shot down near his farm was nicknamed *Picklepuss*. Its pilot, Captain Robert Knox of the 8th Air Force, is buried in the American Cemetery in Henri-Chapelle. Every year on August 17, Marcel and his wife Mathilde place flowers on Captain Knox's grave. Marcel witnesses another aerial fight above his parents' farm, this time between two fighters. He recalls: "You could see them shooting at each other, one would swoop and shoot at the other, then the other would swoop and shoot at the first. All of a sudden, one of the planes explodes and falls in pieces maybe 300 yards from our house." The German border patrol stationed nearby searches the area. Marcel describes a German soldier with his dog finding a piece of the pilot's body: "He was yelling to his dog: 'Eat! Eat some Brit!' And the dog was biting into the flesh." An officer came running and promptly dressed the soldier down. The tail section of the plane had been found with a swastika on it.

Repple Depples

As soldiers are killed, missing in action or wounded, they are replaced on an individual basis by men drawn from Replacement Depots, or "Repple Depples" as the soldiers know them. While this system makes sense from a logistical standpoint, it has a deplorable effect on morale because it treats soldiers as interchangeable pawns rather than members of cohesive teams with strong bonds of friendship and loyalty. By the end of 1944, casualty figures have risen to alarming levels, both in Europe and in the Pacific. The Battle of the Hurtgen forest alone causes 30,000 casualties. The pool of young American men of draft age is insufficient to maintain the army at full strength. Sprawling Infantry Replacement Training Centers train conscripts fresh out of high school. The very name of these centers is controversial as it reminds these teenage boys and their families that they are about to step into the shoes of dead or grievously injured men. At the end of seventeen weeks of training, sometimes less, the young soldiers slated for Europe are shipped across the Atlantic to the United Kingdom, then across the English Channel to France. From there, they are typically shuffled through a network of replacement depots in old boxcars known as "forty and eights" because of their capacity for forty men or eight horses. William Campbell, then an eighteen-year-old replacement recalls: "There is nothing in the boxcar but a little bit of straw. You were just sitting against your duffle bag." In December 1944 the two largest replacement depots are located in Givet, Belgium, and Neufchateau, France. At these camps, the men listen to orientation lectures, they "zero" their rifle sights and replace lost or missing equipment.

Some Divisions organize receiving stations where experienced soldiers offer common-sense advice such as how to avoid trench foot or booby traps. However, most replacements are thrown directly into combat. The haphazard way in which they have made the journey leaves many of them frazzled and disillusioned. Capt Jack Marshall of the 80th Infantry Division wrote: "They came ten or fifteen at a time. Sometimes they arrived at night. I spoke to them in the dark, and they went into combat.[...] About a third disappeared as missing in action before we saw their orders. After a few days another third were in the hospital – wounded or with trench feet.[93]"

Units complain that well meaning as they are, replacements are so ill-prepared for battle that they put not only themselves, but also their comrades at risk, lest they commit some dangerous blunder. Bill Campbell remembers the day he was introduced to the 28th Infantry Division in the Hurtgen forest. He is assigned to a covered dugout with a new partner by the name of Stockwell. By nightfall, Bill is famished, having not yet eaten that day. While Stockwell ventures out of the dugout to set grenade traps, Bill warms up a small can of ham and eggs over a K-ration box he had set alight. He recalls: "I started hearing these noises. I thought: 'What the hell is that?' And Stockwell comes jumping right down into the hole yelling: 'Close the curtain! Close the curtain! They're shooting at you!'" Charles Miller of the 75th Infantry

Division wrote about a replacement who joined his platoon on a scouting mission in Amonines on January 1, 1945: "We had moved only a short distance into the woods when he fired a shot. Everyone stopped and looked around and, when nothing more happened, I asked him what he had fired at. "Nothing, I caught the trigger on a button on my overcoat". I told him to lock his weapon until he saw something to shoot." Later in the same mission, the platoon comes under fire from a German dugout. Miller continues: "The German was almost directly in front of him but, when I called for him to shoot, he replied: 'I can't, my rifle won't work!' Apparently he forgot to unlock it.[45]"

Battle-hardened veterans often treat replacements with disdain if they don't shun them entirely. Some estimate that replacements are unworthy of their shoulder patch, having not been tested in Normandy, Italy or some other bloody campaign. Others take out their stress and frustration on the green men whom they feel are lower in the pecking order. Yet others, having lost many comrades already, are weary of forming new friendships. Chester Wenc is a nineteen-year old replacement when he is introduced to the 106th Infantry Division. He is simply dropped off at night at a dugout east of St. Vith. Inside, four men he has never met before are huddling together to fight the bitter cold. He recounts: "They didn't say nothing to me. I sat with the four guys and if I asked anything they said: 'Shut you mouth and do as you're told!'"

Casualty rates are high among new replacements. Officers who do not want to risk their most experienced men often assign them the most dangerous missions. Many of them are naively willing to take risks to earn the respect of their outfit. Ostracized, disillusioned and feeling no loyalty to their units, they are more likely to desert, to cower under fire or to succumb to combat fatigue.

Soldiers returning to duty after hospitalization dislike the replacement system as much as anybody. Bill Mauldin wrote: "A soldier's own outfit is the closest thing to a home he has over there, and it's too bad when he has to change unnecessarily.[38]" Rather than being sent to their original units with their buddies, something they desperately want, they are usually incorporated into the flow of new recruits at replacement depots. As they wait for their new assignments, many delight in showing off their wounds and telling horrific war stories to already apprehensive young soldiers. Many hospital returnees choose to go AWOL (Absent without leave) and to rejoin their old unit on their own. Herb Adams of the 82nd Airborne Division was hospitalized for about two months with frozen feet. He remembers: "They wouldn't let me go back to the paratroopers.[...] I got a pass to Paris, and I found out in Paris that some of the guys were on leave from my unit. I was able to come back the second day, got on a truck of the 504th back to where they were camping near Lyon, France."

The purpose of this mimeographed letter (A) is to reassure the family of a new recruit by presenting a convivial image of the Ordnance Replacement Training Center in Aberdeen, Maryland. Photo: Replacements of the 90th Infantry Division are trained in the use of a bazooka somewhere in France in December 1944. U.S. National Archives photo. The acronym IRTC on these two brochures (B) stands for Infantry Replacement Training Center. The inscription on this pin (C) is the motto of the Infantry School in fort Benning, Georgia.

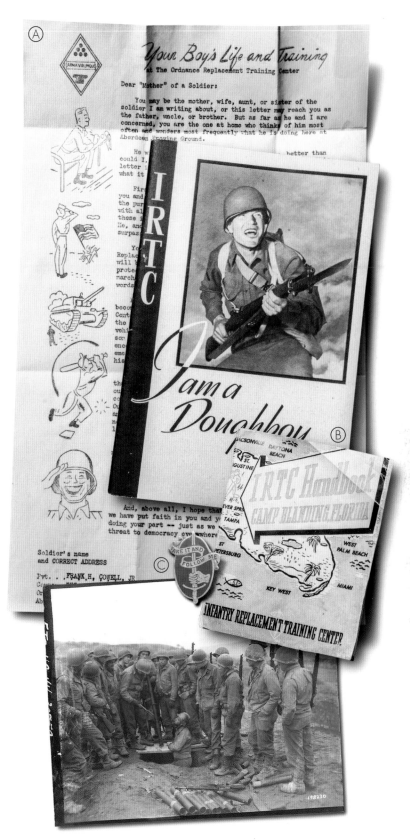

Strains in the Alliance

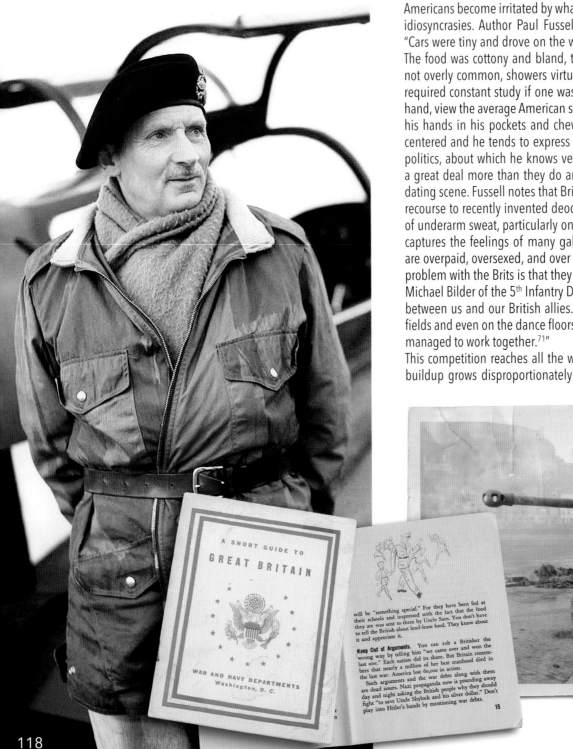

Following America's belated military entry into the war, American troops pour into Great Britain in preparation for the liberation of continental Europe. Close to a million and a half Americans are stationed in southern England, so many that 4,500 new cooks have to be trained to feed them.[94] Welcome as the American military support is, frictions soon start to develop between the "Yanks" and the "Limeys" as they call each other.

Americans become irritated by what they perceive as British snootiness and nonsensical idiosyncrasies. Author Paul Fussell, a Lieutenant in the 45th Infantry Division wrote: "Cars were tiny and drove on the wrong side of the road. Victuals were vastly different: The food was cottony and bland, the beer was soft and lukewarm [...] Bathtubs were not overly common, showers virtually nonexistent.[...] The coinage was irrational and required constant study if one was to avoid being cheated.[95]" The British, on the other hand, view the average American soldier as brash and ill-mannered. He slouches, keeps his hands in his pockets and chews with his mouth open. In conversation he is self-centered and he tends to express strong convictions on subjects such as international politics, about which he knows very little. British soldiers resent the fact that GIs earn a great deal more than they do and the marked advantage that it gives them on the dating scene. Fussell notes that British women are drawn to American soldiers who had recourse to recently invented deodorant, while their British counterparts tend to smell of underarm sweat, particularly on the dance floor. A popular joke of the time perfectly captures the feelings of many galled Brits: "The problem with the Yanks is that they are overpaid, oversexed, and over here." Which prompts the American retort that: "The problem with the Brits is that they are underpaid, undersexed, and under Eisenhower." Michael Bilder of the 5th Infantry Division wrote: "There was a real sense of competition between us and our British allies. This was true in the battle for girls, on the training fields and even on the dance floors. It was so obvious it was almost tangible, yet we still managed to work together.[71]"

This competition reaches all the way up the chain of command. As the Allied military buildup grows disproportionately American, it is placed under the overall command of American General Dwight Eisenhower. The British, who fought the war from the beginning, resent being relegated to a subordinate role. Among the most vocal critics of the American Command is British Field Marshal Bernard Montgomery. "Monty's" victory in El Alamein has made him a national hero. He is revered by soldiers who appreciate his frank and casual demeanor, but he is thoroughly disliked by American Generals who view him as boastful egomaniac and an overly cautious tactician. In a diary entry dated December 27, 1944, General Patton writes: "Monty is a tired little fart. War requires the taking of risks and he won't take them.[96]" Eisenhower himself grows exasperated with Montgomery's disparaging of his American peers and insistence that he should be given overall command of ground forces in Europe. During a conversation, Montgomery displays such lack of tact that Eisenhower is compelled to interject: "Easy Monty, you can't talk to me like that. I'm your boss![95]" Historian and author Antony Beevor advances the hypothesis that Montgomery may have suffered from a form of Asperger syndrome that precluded him from anticipating his interlocutors' emotional responses.[44]

On December 20, because the German salient has cut off the 1st and 9th Armies from General Bradley's headquarters in Luxembourg, Eisenhower temporarily transfers command of all Allied forces north of the Ardennes to Montgomery. Unfortunately, when the news breaks, no mention is made of the temporary nature of the arrangement. This would later irk British newspapers. As they see it, the Americans call Montgomery to the rescue when they are in dire straights, then promptly dismiss him once he has restored the situation. On January 7, Montgomery gives a press conference with the goal of soothing Anglo-American relations. The prepared speech praises Eisenhower and the fighting qualities of American soldiers, stating among other things: "I never want to fight alongside better soldiers." Unfortunately, Montgomery also boasts: "This battle has been most interesting, I think probably one of the most interesting and tricky battles I have ever handled." The overall tone of the speech is patronizing and it gives an inflated impression of British participation. American commanders and Bradley in particular, having been caught off guard by Hitler, are embarrassed and perhaps overly sensitive to criticism. They perceive the speech as yet another attempt by Montgomery to belittle them and to maneuver for an appointment as overall ground commander. Bradley and Patton both inform Eisenhower that they will sooner resign than serve under Montgomery. British Prime Minister Winston Churchill, is dismayed by the rift developing between the two allies. On January 18, 1945, he is prompted to give a speech before the House of Commons in which he states: "Care must be taken not to claim for the British Army an undue share of what is undoubtedly the greatest American battle of the war, and will, I believe, be regarded an ever-famous American Victory."[89]

Left: Field Marshal Bernard Montgomery. Bottom: The War Department distributes various brochures to prepare American soldiers for cultural differences before they are sent to Great Britain. Right: An American-made British Firefly tank guards a Meuse bridge in Namur during the Battle of the Bulge.

The Battle of Lanzerath Ridge

Twenty-year-old Lieutenant Lyle Bouck heads an intelligence and reconnaissance platoon. He is tasked with setting up an observation post overlooking Lanzerath's main road near the Belgo-German border. The position at the edge of woods consists of well concealed dugouts covered with pine logs. Bouck and his men report sounds of heavy tracked vehicle traffic in the Losheim area. In the early morning of December 16, the eastern sky lights up and soon thereafter the area is hit by a heavy artillery barrage. The American armored task force in Lanzerath withdraws, but omits to inform Bouck. Thus, his eighteen-man platoon, later joined by four forward artillery observers, are the only men standing in the path of an entire German division. Bouck observes a column of more than 250 German paratroopers casually approaching from the east, clearly unaware of the American position. Unbeknown to Bouck, these elite German soldiers are tasked with punching a hole through the American lines ahead of Kampfgruppe Peiper's massive panzer force. Bouck is denied permission to withdraw and ordered to hold at all cost. He waits for the bulk of the paratroopers to march within range, but just as he is about to give the order to fire, a young girl emerges from a house to address a German officer as she points in Bouck's direction. Immediately, the German officer yells orders and his paratroopers take cover in the ditches on both sides of the road.[44] The Germans launch several frontal attacks but they are mowed down by the Americans who enjoy a perfect field of fire. Many are picked off as they reach a barbwire fence halfway through the field. At one point, the Americans cease fire to allow German medics waving white flags to pick up the wounded. By dusk, low on ammunition, they are finally flanked, overrun and taken prisoner. Twenty-two Americans have inflicted hundreds of German casualties, and most importantly, they have held off the entire 6th Panzer Army for a full day. Amazingly, only one of Bouck's men died on the Lanzerath ridge. All others including Bouck would survive the war.

Grenades and Grenade Launchers

The MK2 fragmentation grenade (A) is the standard American anti-personnel grenade. The grooved cast iron body earns it the nickname of "pineapple" grenade. Hand grenades come in wooden crates of 25, each packaged in individual cardboard tubes (C). The yellow stripe at the neck indicates that this one is filled with TNT. On average, a soldier is capable of throwing the 1.5 pound MK2 up to 90 feet. Its lethality is limited to a radius of about 15 feet, but it can inflict severe wounds well beyond that range.

The white phosphorus grenade (B), often referred to as "Willy Pete" because of the initials WP, is a smoke, incendiary and anti-personnel grenade. White phosphorus is a highly dangerous and toxic substance that spontaneously combusts in contact with air and emits a dense white smoke. A small bursting charge at the core of the grenade scatters the phosphorus over a 20' radius. Because it melts as it burns and it is nearly impossible to extinguish, white phosphorus sticks to everything, sets fires and causes horrific burns.

Grenades are ignited by a "mousetrap" mechanism. A soldier simply holds the grenade and safety lever together, pulls the pin and throws the grenade. As it leaves the hand, the safety lever is released, freeing a spring-loaded striker that slams into a percussion cap and lights a four to five-second fuse. Grenades ignite with a loud popping sound followed by the hissing and smoking of the fuse. In some cases, this is enough to alert the enemy of the grenade's presence. When used at close range, some soldiers prefer to "cook" the grenade; they count to two or three before throwing the grenade, thus ensuring that the enemy will not have time to throw it back. William Campbell of the 28th Infantry Division remembers that soldiers set up grenade traps to protect the perimeter of their positions at night. They secured them to trees, loosened the pins and attached them to tripwires, or drew strings all the way to their foxholes, so they could set the grenades off remotely.

Two or three riflemen per squadron are equipped with grenade launchers (D) that fit on the muzzle of their rifles, or carbines (E). Thus equipped, and using blank cartridges as propellant (F), they can launch grenades to distances up to 245 yards. Types of rifle grenades include white phosphorus, illuminating (G) and anti-tank (H). Even ordinary fragmentation grenades can be launched with the help of an adapter (I). The velocity of the grenade can be adjusted by sliding it more or less over the graduated launcher. Rifle grenades can be fired from the shoulder, but for high-arching trajectories, it is best to rest the butt of the rifle on the ground and tilt the rifle in the direction of the target. To achieve a precise elevation, an optional sight (J) with a bubble level can be mounted to a dialed bracket (K) screwed onto the stock of the rifle. The sight comes with instructions (L) and a range table printed on waterproof paper.

Anti-tank rifle grenades prove useless against German tanks, but useful in urban fighting. Men of the 30th Infantry Division are clearing Stavelot house by house. U.S. Army photo.

Reading Material for the Troops

Reading is a popular pastime and a convenient escape from the horror or boredom of military life. Cartoonist and veteran Bill Mauldin wrote: "Soldiers at the front read K-ration labels when the contents are listed on the package, just to be reading something. God knows they are familiar enough with the contents.[38]"

Libraries and schools across the United States participate in *Victory Book Campaigns* [97] to collect donated books for the armed forces. Unfortunately, many donors seize the opportunity to get rid of old, less desirable books. Of the 10,827,097 books that are gathered, close to half are deemed unsuitable and sold for scrap paper.[98] The program stocks libraries in military camps, aboard navy ships and in USO clubs (See page 128), but large, hardcover books are impractical for soldiers near combat zones. In 1942, the *Council of Books in Wartime*, an association of publishers, booksellers and authors, launches the *Armed Services Editions* (A) under contract with the War Department. It is a collection of mostly unabridged small-size paperback books. Titles include classic and contemporary novels and non-fictions, with the aim of educating as well as entertaining the soldiers. The Army purchases the books for about 6¢ each and distributes them to soldiers free of charge. So big is the appetite for *Armed Services Editions*, that soldiers who have read the first half of a book, often tear it off and hand it to awaiting buddies. By the end of the program in 1946, the collection has grown to 1,322 titles with 123 million books in print.

Other publishers release their own wartime formats. The *Royce Publishing Company* of Chicago publishes its lowbrow *Quick Reader* collection (B), sized specifically to fit in the front pocket of army shirts.

Above all else, soldiers crave news about the overall progress the war and life back in the United States. John McAuliffe of the 87th Infantry Division explains: "You know nothing. You don't know what the next company is doing, or even the next squad in your platoon. They don't tell you anything." John who was part of a mortar crew recalls that he rarely knew where he was, or even what he was firing at. The Army publishes *Stars and Stripes* (C), an official daily newspaper sporadically handed out along with rations or the mail. Frank Mareska of the 75th Infantry Division wrote: "We were glad to get a copy. We felt that we were back in touch with our home in a way [...] We fell to reading every word in silence before making any comments such was our thirst for news about what was going on or the big picture.'[28]"

Starting in 1942, the Army publishes a magazine titled *Yank, the Army Weekly* (D). Yank articles are written by the soldiers themselves. The magazine has a cover price of 5¢, because it is believed that a free magazine might be perceived as mere propaganda. The most popular feature of Yank is the Pin-up girl page with seductive young movie stars in sexy attire.

Cpl. Norman Beckman of the 490th Armored Field Artillery Battalion reads "Yank" during a lull in firing on January 9,1945. U.S. National Archives photo.

The Trade-Off

Bill Campbell and his buddy Stockwell of the 28th Infantry Division are sharing a frozen foxhole when they are called to their Command Post. An ambulance and two medics with a stretcher are waiting there and a sergeant explains that they are to pick up a man who stepped on a mine. The four men follow the edge of the woods until they reach an open field where the wounded man lies. Engineers have flagged the mines with red ribbons. The four men soon start carrying the injured soldier back on the stretcher. Bill explains: "I had taken a dive a couple of days earlier and kinda hurt my shoulder. And there was this medic who was in charge, he was a buck sergeant. He must have just come back from a rest. He was clean-shaven with a little trimmed mustache and a new uniform. We looked like bums ourselves." Suddenly, an explosion goes off about five hundred feet back. Bill remembers thinking: "Oh, Jesus, somebody else stepped on a mine!" The team looks back and see a puff of black smoke. The sergeant has noticed that Bill is struggling, he asks: "How are you doing, kid?" Bill replies: "Sarge, my left arm is killing me." The two switch sides and the group continue on their way. A second explosion goes off a little closer, then a third, this time so close that the entire crew is tossed to the ground. Bill feels a sharp pain in his shoulder and sees blood running down his arm. He yells: "I'm hit! I'm hit!" A medic crawls over. Bill recalls: "He was poking around and he said: 'You're fine'. I said: 'What about all the blood?' He pointed to the sergeant that was so neat and clean. His head was hanging off to one side, almost torn off. I wake up thinking about that some nights. We finally got back to the tree line. We figured the Germans were shooting mortars and they were finding their range. I wasn't hit. It was part of his body that hit me. I thought for sure I was hit, it stung so bad." Bill concludes: "You wonder if he knew that somebody died rescuing him. He probably never knew. Because I never knew the medic, I never knew the crew, anybody. I went back to my foxhole, I was shaking my head."

Christmas in the Ardennes

In the months leading to the holidays, American families send Christmas cards and parcels to their soldiers overseas. Cookies, oranges, fruitcakes, nuts, candy and chocolate are common gifts. Food is usually shared and consumed as soon as it is received, because soldiers have no practical way to carry the extra weight. Army postal clerks redouble their efforts, but the glut of Holiday mail causes delays. On December 9, 1944, John Duquoin of the 743rd Tank Battalion writes to his mother: "Frankly, I think it's this silly damned Christmas business, which could very well have been dispensed with this year, and for the duration as far as I'm concerned. I'd much rather have my normal mail coming through, than to get nothing at all but samples of everybody else's fruitcake and peanuts." Frederick Smallwood of the 106th Infantry Division receives his first package around the middle of January, and would not receive the last one until April 1st.[41] He recalls: "This was before cling wrap, plastic bags, aluminum foil, scotch tape, or plastic peanuts for packing, etc. All they had to pack with was waxed paper, brown paper, and popcorn for packing. Popcorn worked real well to prevent all the cakes and cookies from being crushed.[41]" If he is lucky, a soldier receives hand knit socks, a hat or a pair of gloves. Unfortunately, most Americans at home cannot imagine just how harsh the living conditions are in the Ardennes. Incongruous gifts such as slippers or aftershave lotion are welcomed with laughter by men in their muddy foxholes. A buddy of Victor Sacco of the 552nd Field Artillery Battalion is perplexed by cans of tomato juice sent to him by his dad, until he notices solder at the bottom. Remembers Victor: "His dad had punched a little hole to take the tomato juice out. Then he had poured whiskey in there and he'd soldered the hole shut."

Soldiers billeted in safe areas such as military hospitals, headquarters, and other bases of operation in the rear, do their best to stir up some Christmas spirit. They set up signs and decorate Christmas trees. If they cannot find ready-made decorations, they use first aid bandages, toilet paper, tin cans, or any other colorful tidbit they find. Instead of tinsel, they use tin foil from cigarette wrappers, or chaff, strips of aluminum foil dropped from airplanes to confuse German radars.

On Christmas, *Voice of America*, the official American radio in Europe, broadcasts President Roosevelt's Christmas greetings: "On behalf of a grateful nation, I send to the men and women of our armed forces everywhere warm and confident wishes this fourth Christmas of war. On Christmas Day more than any other day we remember you with pride and humility, with anguish and with joy. We shall keep on remembering you all the days of our lives. It is, therefore, with solemn pride that I salute those who stand in the forefront on the struggle to bring back to a suffering world the way of life symbolized by the spirit of Christmas." Also broadcast that day, are a Christmas Mass and a lineup of holiday tunes including Bing Crosby's melancholic hit *I'll be home for Christmas* (if only in my dreams).

For many soldiers on the front line, Christmas might have gone completely unnoticed, if it weren't for the Army cooks' attempts to deliver turkey dinners. Bill Campbell of the 28th Infantry Division recalls: "They sent a kitchen up to the front. You wouldn't believe! They were pulled by little donkeys, twenty of them. We saw them coming and they looked like Gypsies." Bill's unit is treated to a warm turkey meal complete with mashed potatoes and cranberry sauce. "And the next day," laughs Bill, "everybody got the shits!" Peter Drevinsky of the 26th Infantry Division remembers that his Christmas dinner was the first warm meal he received in a long time: "It was poultry of some kind. I ate it as if it were turkey. Heaven forbid, we're in the middle of a battle and we get a Christmas meal. You can bet your bottom dollar, the morale really improved!" In most cases, the turkey dinner is little more than symbolic. Sgt Albert Gaydos of the 4th Armored Division recalls his Christmas feast as: "One piece of cold turkey, a Hershey bar, apple and a cigar.[99]" On Christmas Day, Lionel Adda of the 99th Infantry Division is laboriously digging through frozen earth to improve his foxhole. He wrote: "As I looked up, I saw two GIs, tense and with blood-shot eyes, carrying two cans. One of them thrust a small, almost-cold turkey leg into my hand, the other handed me two slices of white bread and a couple of pieces of hard candy. [...] 88-mm shells began falling around us. Almost choking on that first bite, I realized that the Germans were watching those two poor soldiers and harassing them with artillery fire as they delivered our meals. [...] It seemed almost criminal to me that the lives of soldiers could be jeopardized for such an almost meaningless gesture.[100]" Paul Reed of the 17th Airborne Division is in Reims, France on Christmas, well back from the fighting, yet he is disappointed with a Christmas dinner of beans and rice. He emphasizes: "I mean just beans and rice, not even salt.[101]"

If some soldiers manage to find a little bit of peace and merriment on Christmas, for most of them, the day is marked only with some extra homesickness. Preoccupied with survival and dismal weather conditions, they have little time or reason to celebrate. Captain May Alm, a nurse at the 104th Evacuation Hospital reflects a widespread sentiment when she writes: "I was on duty all Christmas Day. No one had time to mention Christmas on that terrible Sunday.[102]"

Walter Prsybyla of the 2nd Infantry Division writes Christmas cards on November 30, 1944 in Heckhalenfeld, Germany. Opposite page: On November 18, 1944, Edmund Dill shares the Christmas treats he just received from his wife with his buddies Carl Anker and Sergeant Ted Bailey.
U.S. National Archives.

VICTORY

from SOMEWHERE IN GERMANY
we wish you a Merry Xmas

Merry Christmas

A MERRY CHRISTMAS AND A HAPPY NEW YEAR

HOLIDAY GREETING STATIONERY
to The Boys in Service
5 SHEETS & 5 ENVELOPES 10¢ 4 BEAUTIFUL COLOR

FOR SENDING PACKAGES TO
U.S. MILITARY and NAVAL PERSONNEL 10¢
24 CAUTION LABELS
No.79 25 PARCEL POST LABELS

HANDLE WITH CARE
RUSH
THIS SIDE UP
FRAGILE HANDLE WITH CARE

A MERRY CHRISTMAS AND A HAPPY NEW YEAR
U.S. ARMY

STAMPS for HEROES
48 STAMPS FOR ONLY 5¢
ARMY

PLACE THESE ON YOUR LETTERS AND PARCELS WHEN YOU SEND THEM WORD FROM HOME!

Hurry Up! THIS IS FOR A SOLDIER
Hurry Up! THIS IS FOR A SOLDIER
Hurry Up! THIS IS FOR A SOLDIER
Hurry Up! THIS IS FOR A SOLDIER

Massacres

Around noon on December 17th, 1944, near Baugnez, Kampfgruppe Peiper's leading elements come upon an American convoy of the 285th Field Artillery Observation Battalion on its way to St Vith. The SS armored vehicles open fire, setting several American trucks ablaze and immobilizing the convoy. Caught by surprise in the open and armed only with rifles and pistols, the Americans are no match for the crack SS Panzergrenadiers. About 130 prisoners are rounded up, stripped of their valuables, cigarettes and gloves and marched to a field alongside the road. Suddenly, an officer takes out his pistol and fires at the prisoners. Machine guns immediately follow suit. The prisoners are mowed down in a matter of seconds. Germans then walk among the dead and the dying, kicking and prodding them with rifles. Those who are still moving or moaning in agony are shot in the head. Some of the prisoners elude death by feigning it, or manage to run into nearby woods. In all, 84 unarmed prisoners are murdered in cold blood. Although the killing takes place in Baugnez, it becomes known as the Malmedy massacre. Peiper's men had already murdered at least 69 American prisoners in Honsfeld and Büllingen that morning.[6]

The same day, eleven black soldiers from the 333rd Field Artillery Battalion who have escaped capture near St Vith, reach the house of the Langer family in Wereth. Having walked for much of the day, they are cold, tired and hungry. The Langers offer them food and a chance to warm up, but an hour later a small detachment of Kampfgruppe Knittel arrives in town and collaborators inform them of the presence of the American soldiers. The Americans, who only have two rifles between them, give themselves up without resisting and are marched off at gunpoint. Later that evening, villagers hear gunshots. The bodies, frozen and half buried in snow, would be recovered six weeks later just as their SS murderers left them. Most have been goaded with bayonets, shot or hit in the head with rifle butts. One man has both legs broken; another man's fingers are nearly cut off. Over the next three days, SS men would murder a further 209 American prisoners of war, mostly in the northern sector of the offensive in towns including Ligneuville, Trois-ponts, La Gleize and Stoumont.[6]

The Germans massacre civilians as well. They have returned to Belgium with SD (Sicherheitdiesnt) intelligence units whose sole purpose is to exact vengeance on partisans and the population that had welcomed the American liberators a few months earlier. On December 21, an SD unit, likely made up of French nationals, rounds up citizens of Bourcy and Noville. They have brought newspaper clippings with articles about the town celebrating the arrival of the American liberators. Frustrated by their failure to identify the people on the photos, they execute the schoolmaster, the priest and five other young men seemingly picked at random. On Christmas Eve, another SD unit arrives in the town of Bande. It is there to avenge German soldiers killed in the area by partisans right before the American liberation. The SS soldiers gather all the men and interrogate them brutally. Then, one by one, the captives are lead through the front door of a burnt-out café. As each enters, he is shot in the back of the neck and pushed into the gaping cellar. Twenty-one-year-old Léon Praile tries in vain to convince other captives to rush their guards. When his turn comes, he punches his guard in the face, jumps over a low wall and takes off running. Shots ring past him, but he manages to escape into the woods. In all, 34 men are executed.[44]

In and around Stavelot, Ster and Parfondruy, Peiper's SS murder at least 164 men, women and children. On December 22, Charles Corbin of the 3rd Armored Division

Right: Medics examine the bodies of victims of the Malmedy massacre they just dug out from the snow. Below: The German MG 34 machine gun. Facing page: War correspondent Jean Marin examines a young victim of the massacre at the Legaye house in Stavelot. U.S. National Archives.

Red Really Hates Germans

Chuck Wenc originally of the 106th Infantry Division is attached to the 36th Army MP Division to guard some 19,000 German prisoners. At first, the prison camp is nothing more than a large open field but eventually, a perimeter fence is erected. Chuck recalls: "The prisoners didn't eat for four or five days at a time. It was really cold. They'd just huddle. Everyday in the morning, a truck would come by and pick up the dead. The prisoners weren't supposed to walk within twenty feet of the fence, or you could shoot them." Instances of prisoners trying to escape are rare until a former sniper known as Red shoots five prisoners in a single night. Chuck explains: "He'd see a German and say: 'Hey, cigarette?' When a German came over and took a cigarette, he'd chat with him while he was smoking, and when he turned and walked away, he'd shoot him. Then a Jeep would come up and he'd say: 'Prisoner tried to escape.' Red was bragging to a guy in the mess hall and telling them what he was doing. The guy reported him to an officer. They called him in and he admitted it. He just hated Germans. They court-martialed him. Instead of sending him to jail, they shipped him out to another company."

is scouting the town of Parfondruy. He wrote: "I entered a house and saw a dead elderly couple, bullet holes in their heads, their throats cut, lying in their blood. Another house had two women and a baby dead in a crib. One of the women was nude with a bullet hole in her head and part of her left arm hacked off. I was at a corner standing in a yard when two children appeared like out of the fog, and said: 'Vive l'Amérique !' One of our soldiers stopped them and told them not to enter the house as the people were dead. They said they were looking for their parents and relatives and went in.[103]"

Twenty-three people take refuge in the basement of the Legaye house in Stavelot. They hear Americans taking position in the house above them and firing from the windows. When the Germans eventually overtake the house, they are surprised to find civilians. They accuse them of helping the Americans and execute them in the front yard. 1st Lieutenant Franck Warnock describes the horrific scene: "A boy of about 8-10 years, wearing no hat, had been smashed in the head by a rifle butt. He lays in a heap with the imprint of the rifle butt clearly showing. I counted 23 dead in an area hardly more than 10 feet by 20 feet.[104]"

In preparing for his Ardennes offensive, Hitler had insisted that: "Troops must act with brutality and show no human inhibition. A wave of fright and terror must precede the troops.[105]" This would prove to be yet another of Hitler's miscalculations. If he succeeds is generating fear among defenseless civilians, the reaction from American soldiers is anger, thirst for revenge and resolve to die fighting rather than surrender. American senior commanders, including General Omar Bradley, tacitly approve acts of retribution.[44] For some time after the Malmedy massacre, Americans routinely shoot SS soldiers trying to surrender. In a diary entry dated January 4, 1945, General Patton writes: "There were also some unfortunate incidents in the shooting of prisoners. I hope we can conceal this.[96]" Patton is probably referring to the Chenogne massacre that has taken place three days earlier: About 60 German prisoners were marched out of town, lined up along a road and machine-gunned in cold blood.

The USO

At the request of President Roosevelt, the United Service Organization is constituted in 1941 by several religious and welfare organizations with the goal of providing recreation and entertainment to boost the morale of servicemen. During the war, more than 3,000 USO clubs are established in major U.S. cities and wherever soldiers are present in large numbers. Hosted by young USO hostesses, they are touted as "homes away from home" where soldiers can relax and partake in leisure activities such as reading, sports, games, crafts, dances, movies, etc. But the USO would be best remembered for its camp shows. Thousands of entertainers perform for soldiers around the world, sometimes perilously close to combat areas. Shows typically feature a mix of music, dance and comedy numbers. They range in sophistication from Hollywood-style extravaganzas featuring hundreds of performers, to what can best be described as street performances.

Through the winter of 1944-45, actor Mickey Rooney presents what he calls *Jeep Shows*. Accompanied by singer Bob Priester and accordionist Mario Pieroni, Rooney performs vaudeville numbers, bits from his movies and imitations of other famous actors. Rooney wrote: "We put up our first show between two Sherman tanks in a Belgian snowstorm, with sixty guys in the audience, three miles from the front, with the sound of howitzers booming in the distance.[106]" Rooney and his crew endure the same living conditions as the men for whom they perform, living on C rations and going for weeks without the opportunity to wash up. Rooney recounts a thwarted performance near Rodange, Luxembourg: "Just as we returned from our jeep with our stuff, me with the electric megaphone and Pieroni with his accordion, a three-star General burst through the door. We all came to attention. He eyed the room with an imperious look and asked what the hell was going on. 'Sir,' I said, 'We're here to do a show for you.' He said: 'Rooney, that'd be just great, except for one thing. We're about to blow the hell out of this headquarters company in just about eight minutes. So if you don't get your ass out of here, it ain't gonna be around anymore.[106]"

Below: Bob Priester, Mickey Rooney and Mario Pieroni perform one of their "Jeep shows" Below right: German-born movie star Marlene Dietrich signs the plaster cast of sergeant Earl McFarland at a hospital in Belgium. U.S. Army photos. Some USO Clubs operate booths that allow soldiers to record voice messages to mail to their family and friends (A).

A bazooka team of the 82nd Airborne Division near Bosson. U.S. Army photo.

M9 "Bazooka" Anti-Tank Rocket Launcher

The anti-tank rocket launcher is nicknamed "bazooka" because it resembles the crude, trombone-like novelty music instrument invented by comedian Bob Burns. The bazooka is the first weapon combining a shaped charge with a shoulder-fired rocket. The bazooka itself is nothing more than a steel pipe with a shoulder stock, crude sight and electric igniter. The rocket is inserted in the rear of the tube where a spring-loaded clamp (A) holds it in place. The wire of the rocket's igniter is connected to an electrical terminal (B). When the operator squeezes the trigger, a small magneto generates enough current to ignite the rocket. The solid propellant produces a violent, almost explosive blast and is entirely consumed before the rocket exits the launcher, thus the operator is mostly protected from the blast. Although the bazooka has a maximum range of 300 yards, the average distance of a successful tank hit is only 55 yards.[107] The M6A1 rocket's high explosive charge is shaped with a hollow, conical space designed to focus the blast onto a small area at the tip of the rocket. On the outside of a vehicle, a successful hit may look like a benign coin-size hole, but the power of the blast sprays shrapnel and molten steel inside the cabin, wounding everyone inside and setting combustibles on fire. A rocket can penetrate up to 75mm of steel armor, but this is rarely sufficient to breach the frontal armor of a German tank. Even if a bazooka crew manages to hit vulnerable parts, such as the wheels, tracks, side or rear, it takes considerable daring and luck to disable a panzer.

The bazooka proves more useful in other roles. In house-to-house fighting, soldiers use a tactic they called "mouse-holing". Rather than entering a building through doors or windows where they may be expected, soldiers blast holes through walls with bazookas, then toss in grenades or rush inside while the occupants are still stunned. During the Battle of the Bulge, eleven soldiers are awarded the Medal of Honor for actions involving the bazooka. This is not so much a measure of the bazookas's effectiveness as it is a measure of the considerable risk the men have to take to use it successfully.

Venereal Diseases

As they displace and concentrate large numbers of young men, wars have always been catalysts for prostitution and venereal diseases. Gonorrhea, commonly referred to as "the clap" and syphilis are the two most dreaded VDs during the war. Untreated, they can cause crippling complications or even death. As late as 1943, their mercury and arsenic-based treatments are almost as harmful as the diseases themselves.

The War Department fears that venereal diseases might become a drain on manpower and medical resources as it had been during World War I. The training of every recruit includes sex education lectures and films. These teach that "easy women" and prostitutes are infected with highly contagious venereal diseases that inevitably bring shame and suffering. The message is reinforced with various poster and pamphlet campaigns, but these do little to curb prostitution which booms wherever soldiers are concentrated. The perils of war foster a devil-may-care outlook and many young soldiers dread the thought of taking their virginity to the grave. Furthermore, European women find the baby-faced GIs very attractive with their generous pay, their good hygiene and their easy access to cigarettes and other much-coveted commodities.

The Army establishes prophylactic stations recognizable by green cross signage, where soldiers can pick up free condoms (A) and prophylactic kits (B). Prophylactic kits include a soap-impregnated cloth and a tube of mercury-based antiseptic ointment to be applied immediately after sexual contact. Henry Mooseker of the 87th Infantry Division recalls that condoms were useful in more ways than one: "They were put to good use keeping matches and cigarettes dry. They were also used to keep the muzzle of our weapon from filling with snow and ice or mud [...]. They sure as hell couldn't be used for anything else.[47]"

Soldiers are periodically subjected to what they call "pecker parades", sometimes as a form of punishment: They are made to line up at attention with their shorts down while a medical officer (AKA "Pecker checker") inspects them for signs of venereal diseases.

In spite of directives to avoid stigmatization, Army nurses do not always take kindly to patients afflicted with venerial diseases. In January 1944, Herb Adams of the 82nd Airborne Division is admitted to a field hospital because of frozen feet. Other patients bothered by the smell of gangrene have wheeled him to another tent. Herb recalls: "I hadn't been there ten minutes and a nurse comes in. She says: 'Turn that ass of yours over!' She stuck a needle into me... Frankly, I thought it had to be the size of my thumb it hurt so damn bad. I reached over and grabbed her by the wrist and she said: 'You're hurting me!' And I said: 'What the hell do you think you did to me?' She said: 'You bastards get clapped up and you come in here and you want me to take care of you?' 'Oh!', I said 'I didn't realize that that's what happened to my feet!' On the bottom of your bunk, you get a chart. She went over and looked 'Oh my god, I'm awful sorry!' she said, 'What are you doing in the VD ward?'"

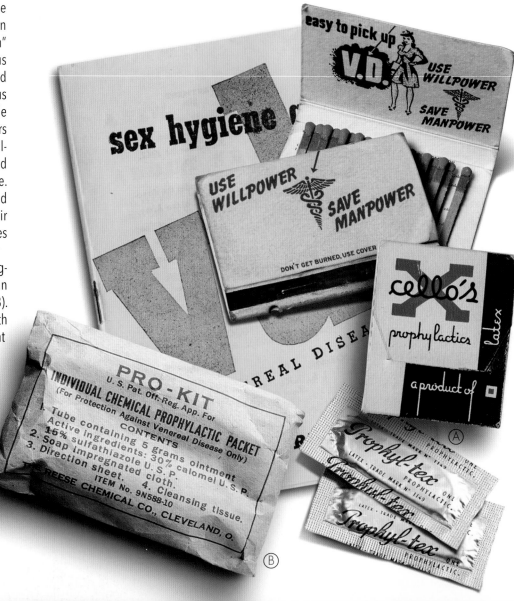

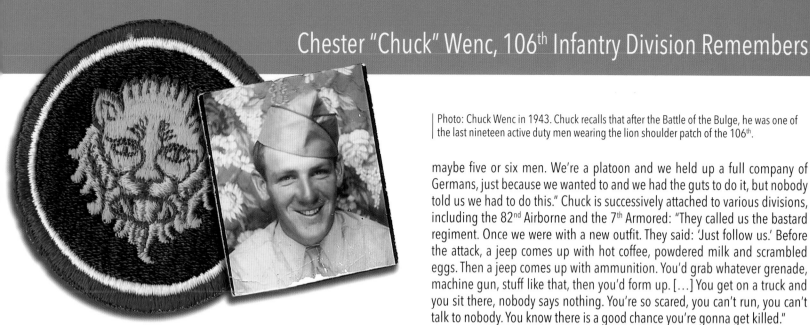

Photo: Chuck Wenc in 1943. Chuck recalls that after the Battle of the Bulge, he was one of the last nineteen active duty men wearing the lion shoulder patch of the 106th.

Wenc Square in Grafton, Massachusetts is named in honor of Chuck's older brother Mitchell, the first citizen of the town killed in World War II. As soon as he can, Chuck volunteers for the Navy, in which his brother had been serving, but he is turned down. After anxiously waiting to be drafted for what seemed to him like an eternity, he goes to his local draft office where he is told that his induction has been delayed on account of his brother's death.

Chuck is inducted on March 2, 1944, the day after his nineteenth birthday. He undergoes six weeks of training at Fort Devens, Massachusetts, followed by another eighteen weeks at Fort McClellan in Alabama where he is formed as a machine gunner and mortar man. He volunteers to become a paratrooper only to find out that a partial dental plate disqualifies him from jump school. On November 13, 1944, he boards a Liberty ship in Newport News, Virginia. Two weeks later he arrives in Naples, Italy, but the ship is quarantined for a further two weeks because a passenger has died of spinal meningitis. Chuck is slated for the Italian front, but when the Battle of the Bulge breaks, he is rushed to Belgium and assigned to the 106th Division. He and his fellow replacements are loaded into trucks one night and disseminated to positions east of St Vith. He finds himself sharing a dark dugout with four soldiers he does not know. He remembers: "If I asked anything they'd say: 'Shut your mouth and do as you're told.'" The 106th is overstretched and hit hard by the 5th Panzer Army. Chuck remembers that everybody dreaded the German Tiger tanks: "If you were in a foxhole you could hear it and you got scared shitless. I saw one and I ducked down. There was another guy behind me. Our holes were maybe a hundred feet apart. The tiger was coming towards us. The tank was over me and I thought: 'Holly Christ!' Then I waited a little while. I popped my head up; he was going away from me. He gets to where the other GI was. He skidded and buried him. The guy was gone."

Some 6,000 men of the 106th are cut off. Out of food and ammunition, they surrender on December 19, but elements of the 424th Infantry Regiment including Chuck, elude capture. Chuck remembers fighting a series of delaying actions: "We fought in groups of maybe five or six men. We're a platoon and we held up a full company of Germans, just because we wanted to and we had the guts to do it, but nobody told us we had to do this." Chuck is successively attached to various divisions, including the 82nd Airborne and the 7th Armored: "They called us the bastard regiment. Once we were with a new outfit. They said: 'Just follow us.' Before the attack, a jeep comes up with hot coffee, powdered milk and scrambled eggs. Then a jeep comes up with ammunition. You'd grab whatever grenade, machine gun, stuff like that, then you'd form up. […] You get on a truck and you sit there, nobody says nothing. You're so scared, you can't run, you can't talk to nobody. You know there is a good chance you're gonna get killed."

During the Battle of the Bulge, Chuck's right hand is injured by a mortar round. Unable to hold a rifle, he temporarily serves as a runner. Chuck is then sent to France to help clean up pockets of German resistance. At one point, his division holds some 19,000 prisoners in a large open field: "They didn't eat for four or five days at a time. It was really cold. They'd just huddle. Everyday in the morning, a truck would come by and pick up the dead."

also notorious for booby trapping their own positions before retreating; they leave mines in their abandoned foxholes, bunkers and vehicles knowing that the Americans are likely take them over. They go so far as to bait minefields with the bodies of American soldiers or their own dead comrades to attract rescuers, grave registry personnel or souvenir hunters. When the body of a dead German soldier is discovered, it becomes customary to tie a long rope around his foot, and drag him from a safe distance to avoid booby-traps.

Shown on this page are a few of the most common German mines. The teller mine 43 (A) is an anti-vehicle mine. The twelve pounds of TNT it contains are sufficient to immobilize a tank or destroy lightly armored vehicles. Metal detectors easily discover the large metallic mines, but they are difficult to disarm. They feature secondary fuse wells on the bottom and side that can be fitted with detonators designed to go off if the mine is displaced in any way.

Victor Sacco of the 552nd Field Artillery is driving near Stolberg,

German Mines and Booby Traps

Understandably, mines hold a particular horror in the mind of the GIs who often prefer the prospect of death to that of a debilitating injury, particularly in the legs or groin area. German forces draw from a wide range of devilishly clever land mines that can be set off by pressure detonators, pull wires or both, and they make very extensive use of them. It is standard practice for Germans to mine the perimeter of defensive positions, particularly the places where one would instinctively run or dive for cover, such as shell holes, ditches, large trees, walls etc.

Reaching mine casualties is perilous. Balancing the need for extreme caution with the impulse to bring urgent care to a soldier in agony is a gut-wrenching experience. Germans are

This engineer undertakes the difficult and dangerous task of neutralizing the mine that his colleague has just found with his metal detector. U.S. National Archives.

Germany on November 23, 1944. He pulls his weapons carrier over to the side of the road to make room for a truck pulling an anti-tank gun painted with the words "Tiger tamer". The truck hits a mine just as it passes by. Victor recounts: "The truck blew up and it picked me right up in my weapons carrier and I landed between the seats where the gear shifter is. My friend, he was on the running board, he flew off and he landed in the gutter. You'd see the guy draped over the side of the (exploded) truck. One guy got out, he was crying, he had tears coming down his eyes. This guy was dead and the truck was blown up."

Among the most dreaded German mines is the Schrapnellmine (B) so named because its main charge is surrounded by ball bearings or steel scraps to increase its lethality. The GIs dub it "bouncing Betty" because rather than exploding underfoot, the S-mine is delayed by a few seconds before it jumps out of the ground and detonates about waist-high. Consequently, rather than affecting a single soldier, a bouncing Betty can potentially kill anybody within a 300 ft radius.

The Schu-mine 42 (C) consists of seven-ounces of TNT and a Bakelite detonator in a small wooden box. It is cheap, easy to mass-produce and hard to detect because it contains very little metal. The Schu-mine is ideal for setting up booby traps. Its relatively small charge rarely kills a man outright, but leaves him grievously wounded, usually with a foot or hand blown off. On December 26, 1944, in Berdorf, Luxembourg, Michael Bilder of the 5th Infantry Division is washing up in an apartment building from which Germans have been repulsed. His sergeant has spotted a pair of manicure scissors sitting in the middle of a table. Bilder recalls: "He reached for the scissors and a large bang followed as he picked them up. The blast took three fingers off the sergeant's hand. The Germans had drilled a tiny hole through the middle of the table and used an almost invisible wire to connect the scissors to a small explosive charge [...] The sergeant simply sat down and started to cry.[71]"

The body of the glassmine 43 (D) is made almost entirely of glass to evade metal detectors. The horrific wounds inflicted by glass shards are difficult to treat because glass is invisible to X-rays. Unlike other types of mines, glass mines are impervious to corrosion. To this day, portions of the Eifel National Park in Germany, just east of the Ardennes are cordoned off because they were sown with glassmines during the war.

"Blue 88s"

The experience of World War I yields contempt for the victims of what is then known as shell shock. They are viewed as cowards that deserve prison if not the death penalty. Many continue to hold that view during World War II. When General Patton visits a military hospital in Italy on August 10, 1943, realizing that a patient has been admitted for a case of nerves, he becomes so angry that he slaps him and threatens him with his pistol as he utters: "I ought to shoot you myself, you goddamned whimpering coward!"[108]

Fortunately, the official stance is more charitable and tends to downplay the condition as "battle fatigue". The term implies that the affliction is benign and easily rectified. At the onset of the war, psychiatrists believe that predisposed men can be screened out of the army. However, experience in the field soon proves that even exemplary soldiers can eventually succumb. This leads the Army to reach a position summed up by the official slogan:"Every man has his breaking point."[109] The stress of combat, injuries, fear, artillery barrages, gruesome scenes and the grief of losing close friends are exacerbated by poor nutrition, lack of sleep and the cold until inevitably, some men reach a breaking point. About one in four evacuations is the result of nervous breakdown. Historian Albert Cowdrey offers the following description:"Intolerable weariness and baseless alarm. Some were stuporous and withdrawn; some tense and violent; some suffered from Parkinson-like tremors or from delusions that mimicked the symptoms of schizophrenia. [...] Weeping, shaking, curling up into the fetal position, or merely numb and unresponsive, they had ceased to be soldiers for a time."[110]

Treatment protocols are developed with the aim of quickly returning as many patients as possible to combat duty. Psychological casualties are segregated to avoid damaging the morale of other patients. They are administered barbiturates orally or intravenously. Blue sodium amytal pills become known as "Blue 88s" supposedly because they knock soldiers out as quickly as the dreaded German 88mm gun. In some cases, psychiatrists interact with sedated patients in an attempt to provoke a cathartic effect. Captain Ben Kimmelman of the 103rd medical battalion recalls:"They would come out of this in, depending on the dosage, 24, 48, 72 hours, and they'd be walking around completely numb. Sometimes they would be slipping and falling. That took a few more hours. And then they would be given a shower, new clothes and a pep talk and the attempt was made to send them back. I say the attempt because it didn't always succeed."[87] The quick process returns about half the men to combat. Many are reassigned to non-combatant roles. Less than 10% are discharged and sent home. Countless veterans who manage to hold on to their sanity to the end of the war, nonetheless suffer psychological injuries that would continue to haunt them for the rest of their lives.

Trophy Hunting

Trophy hunting and trading becomes something of an obsession for many soldiers. Ribbons, hats, medals, decorations, daggers, belt buckles, etc. are eagerly stripped from German bodies or prisoners of war. Objects sporting the SS symbol are particularly sought after, but the German Lugers (A) and P-38 pistols (See page 15) are the most desirable trophies of all. In spite of directives warning them about the dangers of pursuing German souvenirs, some GIs take enormous risks to obtain them. Bob Zelmer and Bill Armstrong of the 26th Infantry Division are on their way to the Ardennes from Metz, France, when they come upon the scene of a battle that has taken place several days earlier. Bill wrote: "We spotted the body of a German officer and walked over to see if his pistol was on him. We thought we saw the butt of it under his body and having heard stories of how the Germans often booby-trapped their own men, I suggested to Bob we get a length of wire from a nearby fence and roll the body over from a distance. Bob had taken but a few step when I yelled: 'Stop, mines!' I had looked down and not six inches from my right foot were the partially exposed fins of an anti-personnel mine. […] I have never been so frightened in my life, then or since. I was actually sick in my stomach. My legs were trembling so that I thought I'd collapse.[…] I promised the good Lord that if I got out of this mess I'd never go souvenir hunting again.[111]"

If the acquisition of enemy souvenirs can be risky, so too is their possession. In case of capture by the enemy, any piece of equipment that can be imagined to have been stolen from a dead comrade often prompts immediate and sometimes fatal retribution. Captain Bruce Crissinger of the 823rd Tank Destroyer Battalion is in La Gleize on December 24 when the 119th Infantry Regiment retakes the town. He wrote: "I was surprised at the venom the infantry showed toward the few German walking wounded still in La Gleize. Anyone with American equipment including boots had to remove it. Several were walking barefoot on a very cold morning.[112]"

Bed Sheet Camouflage

Olive drab uniforms are dangerously conspicuous in snowy landscapes, and white camouflage uniforms are in extremely short supply. The 15,000 British-made snow smocks rushed to the Ardennes are nowhere near sufficient to address the shortage. White bed sheets, tablecloths and curtains are crudely improvised into ponchos, pillow cases are fashioned into helmet covers and strips are wrapped around rifle stocks. Vehicles are whitewashed as are some helmets. When soldiers go door to door collecting bed sheets, most civilians are happy to oblige. One corps reports collecting some 60,000 sheets in a few days. On December 22, 1945, Major John Hanlon of the 502nd Parachute Infantry Regiment appeals to the mayor of Hemroulle near Bastogne. The villagers respond with a pile of about 200 sheets. In 1947, remembering his promise to give the sheets back, and to express his gratitude, he returns to the small community and in a broadly publicized ceremony, distributes some 740 bed sheets he has collected from his hometown of Winchester, MA.

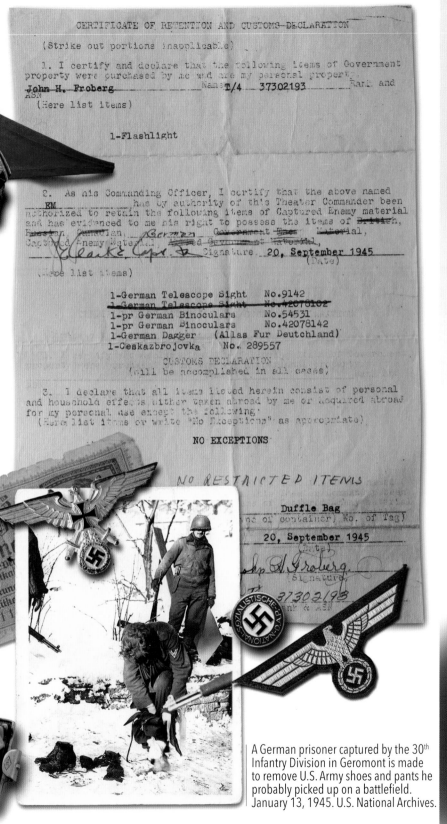

A German prisoner captured by the 30th Infantry Division in Geromont is made to remove U.S. Army shoes and pants he probably picked up on a battlefield. January 13, 1945. U.S. National Archives.

Document shown (Certificate of Retention and Customs Declaration):

CERTIFICATE OF RETENTION AND CUSTOMS DECLARATION

(Strike out portions inapplicable)

1. I certify and declare that the following items of Government property were purchased by me and are my personal property.

John H. Froberg   Name T/4 37302193   Rank and ASN

(Here list items)

    1-Flashlight

2. As his Commanding Officer, I certify that the above named EM has by authority of this Theater Commander been authorized to retain the following items of Captured Enemy material and has evidenced to me his right to possess the items of British, Russian, Canadian, German Government Enemy Material, Captured Enemy Material and German Government Material.

    Clarke Capt. Signature   20, September 1945
    (Date)

(Here list items)

    1-German Telescope Sight   No.9142
    1-German Telescope Sight   No.42078102
    1-pr German Binoculars   No.54531
    1-pr German Binoculars   No.42078142
    1-German Dagger   (Allas Fur Deutchland)
    1-Ceskazbrojovka   No. 289557

CUSTOMS DECLARATION
(Will be accomplished in all cases)

3. I declare that all items listed herein consist of personal and household effects either taken abroad by me or acquired abroad for my personal use except the following:
(Here list items or write "No Exceptions" as appropriate)

    NO EXCEPTIONS

    NO RESTRICTED ITEMS

    Duffle Bag
    (Type of container) No. of Tag)

    20, September 1945
    (Date)

    John H. Froberg
    (Signature)

    T/4 37302193
    Rank & ASN

The Aftermath

The Ardennes are left heavily scarred by the battle. 1,282 civilians are killed,[31] tens of thousands are injured, homeless, or have lost their livelihood. Bitterly contested towns have been shelled and bombed alternatively by both sides. 21,808 buildings are damaged, 5,664 houses are no longer habitable.[31] Towns like Houffalize, Manhay, St Vith, Noville, La Roche, and Clervaux have been all but wiped out. Railroads, bridges and utility lines have been destroyed. Roads are blocked by heavy snow, mines, collapsed buildings and trees, or wrecked military vehicles. Hundreds of communities are cut off with no possibility of trucking in supplies, or evacuating the wounded. The population lives without electricity or running water, eating root vegetables and slaughtering injured farm animals. They sift through the rubble of their homes to salvage what little they can: food, clothing, documents, photos, tools and utensils. Entire towns gather in the few buildings that remain standing, they try to keep warm in cellars, or attempt to patch together some livable space with reclaimed construction material. Dysentery and pulmonary diseases thrive in the cramped, unsanitary conditions. Some communities take to baking their clothes in bread ovens to combat lice infestations.[31]

Civil Affair detachments of the U.S. Army play an important role in initiating reconstruction efforts and shoring up the morale of the locals. They transport displaced people, and deliver food, blankets and emergency supplies. Army medics and nurses treat civilians or provide ambulance transport. Army engineers clear debris and disabled vehicles. They build temporary bridges and remove mines and other dangerous ordnance.

As the snow recedes at the end of the winter, the dead bodies of thousands of soldiers and farm animals are revealed. The acrid smells of burnt wood, masonry, rubber, phosphorus and flesh, give way to the smell of decomposing corpses. Dead Germans are dragged into mass graves. Dead Americans under the care of Grave Registration squads, are buried in temporary cemeteries. Some of them will be returned to the United States at the request of their families, but most will eventually be transferred to the Henri-Chapelle American Cemetery or the Ardennes American Cemetery in Neuville-en-Condroz, where the most recent grave is that of Sgt John T. Puckett or the 99th Infantry Division, whose remains are recovered near Elsenborn in 1992.

Many areas are strewn with rifles, ammunition, grenades, mines and explosives of all sorts. In the eight months following the battle, Belgian bomb removal squads neutralize 5,800 tons of ordnance, including 114,000 land mines.[31] 102 soldiers die and 234 are wounded in the process.[113]

In defiance of the law, some Belgians stash away weapons in the hope of selling them one day, or using them for hunting or perhaps in case they need to join the resistance again in some future conflict. War relics prove irresistible to young boys and teenagers fascinated with weaponry. They imitate their American heroes, explore disabled military vehicles and play with dangerous explosives. In the area of Bastogne, land mines and explosives to kill bout 40 people in the first five months of 1945. [31]

In heavily hit areas, agricultural activities are severely curtailed. An estimated 29,000 farm animals have been killed or are missing. During the liberation in the fall of 1944, retreating Germans have stolen most of the draft horses that are indispensable to small family farms. During the battle, cows and pigs are trapped in burning barns or escape from shell-damaged stalls, or from fences torn down by passing tanks. They wander into minefields, are killed by mistake or shot deliberately by hungry soldiers. Large sections of forest become unsuitable for lumber production because the trees are damaged and peppered with bullets and shrapnel. This in turn, hampers the crucial production of coal for lack of mining timber.

Poor families attempt to salvage what they can from the battlefields. Military coats are dyed and reused. Silk parachutes are turned into bed sheets, shirts, wedding dresses or souvenir handkerchiefs to be sold to American soldiers. Helmets are used as buckets, scoops and troths. Military vehicles are dismantled and stripped of anything useful or valuable, such as tools, tires, seats, motors, etc. Steel from vehicles and brass from spent cartridges are sold for scrap.

Belgian governmental agencies along with humanitarian organizations such as the Red Cross and the Secours d'Hivers distribute clothing, blankets, medical supplies, and provide sanitation guidelines to ward off epidemics.

The spring of 1945 is precocious and warm. Rows of cabins built of wooden planks and tar paper temporarily house families that have lost their homes. German prisoners of war are put to work clearing rubble. With much of the debris removed, the fear of mines diminishing and the arrival of warm weather, reconstruction gains momentum and the population's morale improves. The Belgian government's "Fond National de Secours aux Sinistrés" (the National fund for assistance to war victims) indemnifies citizens whose property has been lost or damaged in the war, but filing is a drawn-out process and reparations are based on prewar property values.

Today, the few remaining wrecked military vehicles have long been erected as monuments in the centers of vibrant towns. The initiated can point out bullet pockmarks on stone houses, and slight depressions left by old foxholes or bomb craters, but it is otherwise hard to imagine that such idyllic and peaceful countryside witnessed one of the war's biggest and bloodiest battles.

Belgian earth is heavy with evocative vestiges of the Battle of the Bulge. Bottom photo: The town of Houffalize is left almost entirely destroyed in the spring of 1945. Nowadays, the German Panther tank that had rolled over into the Ourthe river, has been erected as a monument in the town center. Top photo: This postcard illustrates the start of reconstruction in 1946. Wooden barracks visible on the bottom right, temporarily house homeless inhabitants. Photos from the Thibaut Westhof collection.

Sources

1 - *Quand les conflits troublent la paix de nos vallées* by "Hèyeûs d'sov'nis"

2 - *A General's Life: An Autobiography* by Omar Nelson Bradley and Clair Blair

3 - *The Deserters: A Hidden History of World War II* by Charles Glass

4 - *The Bulge: Per the 146th Engineer Combat Bn. 1944* by Wesley Ross, www.battleofthebulgememories.be

5 - *A Blood-Dimmed Tide: The Battle of the Bulge by the Men Who Fought It* by Gerald Astor

6 - *The Ardennes: Battle of the Bulge* by Hugh M. Cole.

7 - *To Hell and Back, the classic memoir of World War II by America's most decorated soldier* by Audie Murphy

8 - *Ardennes-Alsace* by Roger Cirillo

9 - *The Damned Engineers* by Janice Holt Giles

10 - *Bitter December* by Joseph Kiss, Bulge Bugle February 1993

11 - *The night before Christmas, Bastogne 1994* by Jack T. Prior, Bulge Bugle November 2006

12 - *Patton at the Battle of the Bulge: How the General's Tanks Turned the Tide …* by Leo Barron

13 - *American Military History, Volume 2. The Unites States Army in a Global Era, 1917-2003* by Richard W. Stewart, editor, Center for Military History, United States Army Washington, D.C., 2005

14 - *No Ordinary Time: Franklin & Eleanor Roosevelt: The Home Front in World War II* by Doris Kearns Goodwin

15 - *GI: The American Soldier in World War II* by Kennett, Lee

16 - *Doing Battle, the making of a skeptic* by Paul Fussell

17 - *War and Postwar Wages, Prices, and Hours 1914-23 and 1939-44* United States Department of Labor, Bureau of Labor Statistics.

18 - *History of Combat Pay, Institute for Defense Analysis* by Brandon R. Gould, Project Leader and Stanley A. Horowitz, Task Leader

19 - *The Night Mickey Did Not Get Shot* by Ralph Schip, Memorable Bulge Incidents, 1994

20 - *American Military History Volume II - The United States Army in a Global Era, 1917-2003* by Richard W. Stewart

21 - *Eating for Victory: Food Rationing and the Politics of Domesticity* by Amy Bentley

22 - *A soldier's Odyssey to remember our past as it was* by Frank Moresca

23 - *Souvenirs d'une liégeoise sous les V1* by Marie-Thérèse Hanot

24 - *Valeureux liégeois Sous les Bombes V* by Lambert Graillet

25 - *Operation Paperclip: The Secret Intelligence Program that Brought Nazi Scientists to America* by Annie Jacobsen

26 - *World War II Weapons* by Arnold Ringstad

27 - *FM 5-15 war department field manual corps of engineers field fortifications*

29 - *With CC B / 4th Armored Division in the Bulge* by John Di Battista, www.battleofthebulgememories.be

30 - *Memorable Experience* by Rocco Moretto www.battleofthebulgememories.be

31 - *La Bataille des Ardennes, la vie brisée des sinistrés* by Mathieu Billa, Racine, 2015

32 - *Ernie's War: The Best of Ernie Pyle's World War II Dispatches* by Ernie Pyle.

33 - *Inferno* by Max Hastings

34 - *Where was the Air Force?* by Paul Priday, Bulge Bugle November 2005

35 - *Air Power in the Battle of the Bulge: A Theater Campaign Perspective* by Col William Carter, Airpower Journal, winter 1989

36 - www.87thinfantrydivision.com

37 - *The War Journal of Corporal Jack Graber*

38 - *Up Front* by Bill Mauldin

39 - Archives of the Belgian *Institut Royal de Météorologie*

40 - *Bastogne* by John Cipolla, Bulge Bugle November 2012

41 - *My War* by Frederick Smallwood, www.battleofthebulgememories.be

42 - *Close Contact with the Germans* by Raymond Wenning, Bulge Bugle August 2013

43 - *A Soldier Remembers* by Ray Huckaby, Bulge Bugle February 2008

44 - *Ardennes 1944, The Battle of the Bulge* by Antony Beevor

45 - *In the Battle of the Bulge* by Charles Miller, Bulge Bugle February 1991

46 - *I was with the 508th Paratroop Infantry* by Allan Stein, Bulge Bugle August 1991

47 - *Christmas 1944* by Henry Mooseker, Bulge Bugle February 2005

48 - *Ernie Pyle's War* by James Tobin

49 - *The Execution of Private Slovik* by William Bradford Huie

50 - *Conduct Unbecoming: Fifteen Military Criminals, Rogues and Victims of Justice from the Revolutionary War to Vietnam* by Scott Baron and James Wise, Jr

51 - *Eisenhower, a Soldier's Life* by Carlo D'Este

52 - *The Road to Victory: The Untold Story of World War II's Red Ball Express* by David P. Colley

53 - *American Enterprise in Europe: The Role of the SOS in the Defeat of Germany* by Randolph Leigh and Dwight D. Eisenhower

54 - *Operation Greif and the Trial of the "Most Dangerous Man in Europe"* Western Illinois Historical Review by Adam Bednar Vol. 1 Spring 2009

55 - *I Was There… At the Battle of the Bulge* by Paul Reed, Thunder From Heaven, April 2000

56 - *Malmedy, Belgium Mistaken Bombing, 23 and 25 December 1944* Report by Royce L. Thompson, European Section, OCMH. 5 June 1952

57 - www.malmedy.be, official website of the city of Malmedy

58 - *Medical Department, United States Army Personnel in World War II, Office of the*

Surgeon General Department of the Army, Washington, DC, 1963

59 - *I was a Medic during the Bulge* by Richard Roush, Bulge Bugle August 1990

60 - *Medics in the Bulge* by Ralph Storm, www.battleofthebulgememories.be

61 - Smithsonian National Postal Museum, www.postalmuseum.si.edu

62 - *All Hell Broke Loose* by Donald Schoo, Bulge Bugle August 2014

63 - *The Price of Freedom* by Lynn Aas, www.battleofthebulgememories.be

64 - *One Day of Battle at Houyire Hill January 3, 1945* by Richard Stone

65 - *Government Issue* by Henri Paul Enjames

66 - *The Weather on 16 December 1944* by Donald Bein

67 - *No purple heart for bee sting* by Henry Mooseker, Bulge Bugle February 2006

68 - *Personal Reminiscences of the Retaking of Grandmenil* by Robert Kauffman, www.battleofthebulgememories.be

69 - *The 94th Infantry Division 301st Infantry Regiment at Orscholz* by Eddie Maul

70 - *Fighting for America: Black Soldiers - the Unsung Heroes of World War II* by Christopher Paul Moore

71 - *A Foot Soldier for Patton: the Story of a "Red Diamond Infantryman with the U.S. Third Army"* by Michael Bilder

72 - *Two Fronts, One War* by Charles W Sasser

73 - *My own Battle of the Bulge* by Gus Blass

74 - *Blood for Dignity: The Story of the First Integrated Combat Unit in the U.S.*, by David P. Colley

75 - *Taste of War: World War II and the Battle for Food* by Lizzie Collingham

76 - *The Great Starvation Experiment: Ancel Keys and the Men Who Starved for Science* by Todd Tucker

77 - *War Years 1941-1945 with 327th Field Artillery Bn.* by Lt David Gregg

78 - *Remembering Another Enemy: Cold Weather* by Reuel Long, Bulge Bugle August 2007

79 - *Before Their Time: A Memoir* by Robert Kotlowitz

80 - *Our First Close-up Encounter* by Armand Boisseau, Bulge Bugle February 2006

81 - *Life on the Frozen Tundra* by Kenneth Yockey, Bulge Bugle February 2011

82 - *A Soldier's Month in the Ardennes* by James Cullen

83 - *Technology of War* by Robin Cross

84 - *The Battle of the Ardennes, Malmedy, Belgium*, 16 December 1944 – 23 January 1945 by Frank Towers, www.30thinfantry.org

85 - *"F" Company, 119th Infantry at Neufmoulin's Bridge, 18-19 December 1944* by 1st Lt Edward Arn

87 - *American Experience. The Battle of the Bulge: World War II's Deadliest Battle.* Television Documentary directed by Thomas Lennon and Mark Zwonitzer, 1988

88 - *How to wear a foxhole* by Hugh Rous, Bulge Bugle May 1992

89 - *World War II: Battle of the Bulge* by C. David North

90 - *Combat Infantryman's Memoirs of World War II* by Norval Williams

91 - *Rapport sur le pillage effectué par les troupes américaines à Bastogne* by Mayor Léon Jacquemin

92 - *Belgians Charge Looting by Yanks*, newspaper clipping, Associated Press, 25 January 1944

93 - *Echoes of Distant Battles* par Jack Marshall, Bulge Bugle March 2006

94 - *The War* by Geoffrey C. Ward

95 - *The boys' crusade* by Paul Fussell

96 - *The Patton papers: 1940-1945* by Martin Blumenson

97 - *When Books Went to War: The Stories That Helped Us Win World War II* by Molly Guptill Manning

98 - *M.L.A. Quarterly*, Volumes 5-8, Missouri Library Association, 1944

99 - *25 Days* by Albert Gaydos, Bulge Bugle November 2007

100 - *Grateful For the Small Things* by Lionel Adda, Bulge Bugle November 1993

101 - *I Was There… At the Battle of the Bulge* by Paul Reed, Thunder from Heaven, April 2000

102 - *A Christmas that Wasn't Christmas* by May Alm, Bulge Bugle February 2009

103 - *Civilian Massacre at Parfondruy* by Charles R. Corbin

104 - *The story of a small town in Belgium, Stavelot* by 1st Lt Franck Warnock

105 - *The Guns at Last Light: The War in Western Europe, 1944-1945* by Rick Atkinson

106 - *Life Is Too Short* by Mickey Rooney

107 - *Bazooka vs Panzer: Battle of the Bulge 1944* by Steven J. Zaloga, Alan Gilliland

108 - *Patton, a Biography* by Alan Axelrod and Wesley K. Clark

109 - *Psychological and Psychosocial Consequences of Combat and Deployment with Special Emphasis on the Gulf War* by David H. Marlowe

110 - *Fighting For Life* by Albert E. Cowdrey, www.battleofthebulgememories.be

111 - *Memories of the Battle of the Bulge* by Bill Armstrong, Memorable Bulge Incidents, 1994

112 - *24 Hours, a Prisoner of the Waffen SS* by Bruce Crissinger, Bulge Bugle August 1998

113 - *Ardennes 44, édition 2013: La dernière offensive allemande* by Pierre Stéphany

114 - *A Soldier's Story* by Omar Bradley.

115 - *The U.S. Army in the Occupation of Germany: 1944-1946* By Earl Frederick Ziemke

116 - *Snow and Steel: The Battle of the Bulge, 1944-45* By Peter Caddick-Adams

Acknowledgments

Many thanks to the people and organizations that provided their expertise and access to their collections. Special thanks to my friend Christian de Marcken and to the other eyewitnesses and veterans that accepted to relive painful memories. This book could not have been created without their help and encouragement.

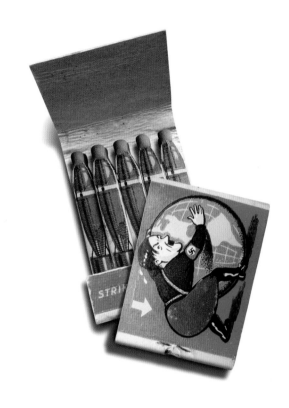

Herbert & Beverly Adams
Anthony Adamsky
Manfred Brülls
Bill Campbell
Paul Campbell
Louis Carbone
Randy Cook
Matthieu Courtoy
Doug Culver
Dr. Michael Culver
Christian & Jeanne de Marcken
Peter Drevinsky

Brian Dugrenier
Jean-Marie Durlet
Ned Froberg
Bill & Betty Gast
Francis Gaudere
Pierre Godeau
Robert Gouvea
Benoit Hambucken
Jean Hambucken
Gordon Hatch
Mike Hashem
Vincent Heggen

Elvire Herbillon
Casey Hogan
Nora Holt
Philippe Krings
Athanace Landry
Michelle Landry
Albert Mark
Roger Marquet
Judie Mason
Dr. John McAuliffe
Charles & Georgette Mernier
Jean-François Noirhomme

Mat Payson
Marcel & Mathilde Schmetz
Robert Stella
Victor Sacco
Dorothy Taft-Barre
John Warner
Harold Ward
Claude Warzée
Chester Wenc
Rodney & Donna Wenc
Thibaut Westhof
Alphonse York

Layouts and photography: Denis Hambucken
Texts: Denis Hambucken

www.racine.be
Subscribe to our newsletter and receive notifications of our new publications and activities

© Éditions Racine, 2017
Tour et Taxis, Entrepôt royal
86C, avenue du Port, BP 104A ● B - 1000 Bruxelles

D. 2017, 6852. 14
Dépôt légal : août 2017
ISBN 978-2-39025-008-1
Imprimé en Slovénie